DIABETIC AIR FRYER COOKBOOK

1200 Days of Mouthwatering & Easy Recipes to Manage Diabetes While Tasting Delicious Food and Care Your Well-Being

WRITTEN BY:

JENNIFER MASON

© Copyright 2023 - All rights reserved.

The content contained within this book may not be reproduced, duplicated or transmitted without direct written permission from the author or the publisher.

Under no circumstances will any blame or legal responsibility be held against the publisher, or author, for any damages, reparation, or monetary loss due to the information contained within this book. Either directly or indirectly.

Legal Notice:

This book is copyright protected. This book is only for personal use. You cannot amend, distribute, sell, use, quote or paraphrase any part, or the content within this book, without the consent of the author or publisher.

Disclaimer Notice:

Please note the information contained within this document is for educational and entertainment purposes only. All effort has been executed to present accurate, up to date, and reliable, complete information. No warranties of any kind are declared or implied. Readers acknowledge that the author is not engaging in the rendering of legal, financial, medical or professional advice. The content within this book has been derived from various sources. Please consult a licensed professional before attempting any techniques outlined in this book.

By reading this document, the reader agrees that under no circumstances is the author responsible for any losses, direct or indirect, which are incurred as a result of the use of information contained within this document, including, but not limited to, errors, omissions, or inaccuracies.

Table of Contents

Introduction 8
    Causes of Diabetes and Risk Factors 8
    Signs and Symptoms of Diabetes 9

Chapter 1. Type 1 and Type 2 Diabetes 10
    What Happens When a Person Has Diabetes? 10
    Types of Diabetes 10
    Foods to Eat 11
    Foods to Avoid 13

Chapter 2. Breakfast 16
    1. Strawberries Oatmeal 16
    2. Tuna Sandwiches 17
    3. Garlic Potatoes with Bacon 18
    4. Chicken & Zucchini Omelet 19
    5. Tomatoes and Swiss Chard Bake 20
    6. Shrimp Frittata 21
    7. Zucchini Fritters 22
    8. Chicken Omelet 23
    9. Scrambled Eggs 24
    10. Almond Crust Chicken 25
    11. Mushroom Cheese Salad 26
    12. Shrimp Sandwiches 27
    13. Mushrooms and Cheese Spread 28
    14. Lemony Raspberries Bowls 29
    15. Asparagus Salad 30
    16. Zucchini Squash Mix 31
    17. Bacon-Wrapped Filet Mignon 32
    18. Pumpkin Pancakes 33
    19. Onion Omelet 34
    20. Sweetened Breakfast Oats 35

Chapter 3. Recipes for Lunch 36
    21. Easy Rosemary Lamb Chops 36
    22. Greek Lamb Chops 37
    23. Easy Beef Roast 38

24. Juicy Pork Chops 39
25. Tuna and Spring Onions Salad 40
26. Bacon-Wrapped Filet Mignon 41
27. Classic Beef Jerky 42
28. Flavorful Steak 43
29. BBQ Pork Chops 44
30. Crispy Meatballs 45
31. Juicy Steak Bites 46
32. Lemon Garlic Lamb Chops 47
33. BBQ Pork Ribs 48
34. Herb Butter Rib-Eye Steak 49
35. Honey Mustard Pork Tenderloin 50
36. Simple Beef Sirloin Roast 51
37. Seasoned Beef Roast 52
38. Beef Burgers 53
39. Season and Salt-Cured Beef 54
40. Simple Beef Patties 55

Chapter 4. Recipes for Dinner 56
41. Brine-Soaked Turkey 56
42. Oregano Chicken Breast 57
43. Thyme Turkey Breast 58
44. Chicken Drumsticks 59
45. Lemon Chicken Breasts 60
46. Parmesan Chicken Meatballs 61
47. Easy Italian Meatballs 62
48. Buttered Salmon 63
49. Crispy Haddock 64
50. Miso Glazed Salmon 65
51. Ground Chicken Meatballs 66
52. Lemony Salmon 67
53. Crispy Tilapia 68
54. Vinegar Halibut 69
55. Crusted Chicken Drumsticks 70
56. Spiced Tilapia 71
57. Simple Haddock 72

58.	Breaded Cod	73
59.	Spicy Catfish	74
60.	Tuna Burgers	75

Chapter 5. Vegetarian Recipes 76

61.	Delicious Air Fryer Cauliflower	76
62.	Spinach Quiche	77
63.	Yellow Squash Fritters	78
64.	Eggplant Parmigiana	79
65.	Air Fryer Brussels Sprouts	80
66.	Endives with Bacon Mix	81
67.	Creamy Potatoes	82
68.	Creamy Cabbage	83
69.	Asparagus & Parmesan	84
70.	Walnut & Cheese Filled Mushrooms	85
71.	Chard with Cheddar	86
72.	Herbed Tomatoes	87
73.	Spiced Almonds	88
74.	Leeks	89
75.	Asparagus	90
76.	Lemony Lentils with "Fried" Onions	91
77.	Cauliflower Steak	92
78.	Onion Green Beans	93
79.	Green Beans and Cherry Tomatoes	94
80.	Onion Soup	95

Chapter 6. Seafood Recipes 96

81.	Grilled Sardines	96
82.	Crunchy Air Fryer Fish	97
83.	Tuna Zucchini Melts	98
84.	Buttery Cod	99
85.	Breaded Coconut Shrimp	100
86.	Codfish Nuggets	101
87.	Easy Crab Sticks	102
88.	Fried Catfish	103
89.	Zucchini with Tuna	104
90.	Deep-Fried Prawns	105

91.	Monkfish with Olives and Capers	106
92.	Salmon with Pistachio Bark	107
93.	Easy Prawn Salad	108
94.	Fried Fish Fingers	109
95.	Salmon with Mushrooms and Bell Pepper	110
96.	Cod and Chicken Broth	111
97.	Spinach with Tuna Fish	112
98.	Sweet Potato with Tilapia	113

Chapter 7. Snacks ... 114

99.	Tacos Crispy Avocado	114
100.	Apple Chips With Cinnamon and Yogurt Sauce	115
101.	Mozzarella Cheese Bites with Marinara Sauce	116
102.	Spanakopita Bites	117
103.	Vegan-Friendly Kale Chips	118
104.	Light Air-Fried Empanadas	119
105.	Whole-Wheat Air-Fried Pizzas	120
106.	Zucchini Chips	121
107.	Air-Fried Avocado Fries	122
108.	Chicken Nachos with Pepper	123
109.	Dark Chocolate and Cranberry Granola Bars	124
110.	Bacon Muffin Bites	125
111.	Brussels Sprout Chips	126
112.	Herbed Parmesan Crackers	127
113.	Cauliflower Crunch	128
114.	Lemon Pepper Broccoli Crunch	129
115.	Delicate Garlic Parmesan Pretzels	130
116.	Cucumber Chips	131

Chapter 8. Dessert Recipes ... 132

117.	Chocolate Mug Cake	132
118.	Chocolate Soufflé	133
119.	Chocolate Cake	134
120.	Choc Chip Air Fryer Cookies	135

Conclusion ... 136
Index ... 137

Introduction

Diabetes is a disease in which blood glucose, also called blood sugar, doesn't get properly regulated. Glucose is the form of sugar that's used by all cells for energy. In diabetes, the body either doesn't produce enough insulin or can't use the insulin that's produced. This a type of disease that occurs when the pancreas can't produce enough insulin, a hormone that is used to help cells use glucose (sugar) for energy. Diabetics must monitor their glucose levels regularly and take insulin to make sure the glucose stays within the normal range.

Diabetes symptoms include excessive thirst, frequent urination, hunger, blurred vision, unexplained weight loss, and sudden numbness or weakness of the arms or legs. Diabetics also experienced excessive sweating, itching, and a dry mouth.

Diabetes is also a disease associated with blood sugar i.e., the concentration of sugar in the blood that the body is unable to maintain within normal limits.

Hyperglycemia occurs when blood glucose exceeds 100 mg./dl fastings or 140 mg/dl two hours after a meal. This condition may depend on a defect in function or a deficit in the production of insulin, the hormone secreted by the pancreas, used for the metabolism of sugars and other components of food to be transformed into energy for the whole organism (such as petrol for the engine).

When blood glucose levels are twice equal to or greater than 126 mg./dl, diabetes is diagnosed. High blood glucose levels—if not treated—over time, lead to chronic complications with damage to the kidneys, retina, nerves peripheral, and cardiovascular system (heart and arteries).

Causes of Diabetes and Risk Factors

Although some of the causes are completely unclear, even trivial viral infections are recognized, which can affect insulin-producing cells in the pancreas, such as:

- Measles.
- Cytomegalovirus.
- Epstein-Barr.
- Coxsackievirus.

For type 2 diabetes, however, the main risk factors are:

- Overweight and obesity.
- Genetic factors: family history increases the risk of developing type 2 diabetes.
- Ethnicity: the highest number of cases is recorded in the populations of sub-Saharan Africa and the Middle East and North Africa.
- Environmental factors are especially related to incorrect lifestyles (sedentary lifestyle and obesity).
- Gestational diabetes, which is diabetes that happens during pregnancy.
- Age: type 2 diabetes increases with increasing age, especially above the age of 65.
- Diet high in fat promotes obesity.
- Alcohol consumption.

- Sedentary lifestyle.

Signs and Symptoms of Diabetes

Symptoms of the disease, which depend on blood sugar levels, are:

- Polyuria, i.e., the high amount of urine production even during the night (nocturia).
- Polydipsia (an intense feeling of thirst).
- Polyphagia (intense hunger).
- Dry mucous membranes (the body's need to replenish fluids and severe dehydration).
- Asthenia (feeling tired).
- Weight loss.
- Frequent infections.
- Blurred vision.

In type 1 diabetes they manifest rapidly and with great intensity. In type 2 diabetes, on the other hand, symptoms are less evident, develop much slower, and may go unnoticed for months or years. Diagnosis often occurs by chance, on the occasion of tests done for any reason: the finding of a glycemia greater than 126 mg/dl allows the diagnosis of type 2 diabetes, which must be confirmed with a second dosage of glycemia and HbA1c.

Chapter 1. Type 1 and Type 2 Diabetes

Diabetes is a common disease that leads to metabolic disorders of carbohydrates and water balance.

As a result, pancreatic functions are impaired. It is the pancreas that produces an important hormone called insulin.

Insulin regulates the level of blood sugar that is supplied with food. Without it, the body cannot convert sugar into glucose, and sugar starts accumulating in the body of a person with the disease.

Apart from the pancreas disorders, the water balance is impaired as well. As a result, the tissues do not retain water, and the kidneys excrete much fluid.

What Happens When a Person Has Diabetes?

When the condition develops, the body produces too little insulin. At the same time, the level of blood sugar increases, and the cells become starved for glucose, which is the primary source of energy.

Types of Diabetes

There are two types of diabetes.

Type 1 Diabetes

This condition is also known as insulin-dependent. It usually affects young people under 40. People with type 1 diabetes will need to take insulin injections for the rest of their lives because their body produces antibodies that destroy the beta-cells which produce the hormone.

Type 1 diabetes is hard to cure. However, it is possible to restore pancreatic functions by adhering to a healthy diet. Products with a high glycemic index such as soda, juice, and sweets should be excluded.

Type 2 Diabetes

This happens as a result of the lack of sensitivity of the pancreas cells towards insulin because of the excess of nutrients. People with excess weight are the most susceptible to the disease.

Difference

	Type 1	Type 2
Whom It Affects	Represent up to 5–10 % of all cases of diabetes. It was once called "juvenile-onset" diabetes because it was thought to develop most often in children and young adults. We now know it can occur in people of any age, including older adults.	Accounts for 90–95 % of all diagnosed cases of diabetes. It used to be called "adult-onset" diabetes, but it is now known that even children—mainly if they're overweight—can develop type 2 diabetes.

What Happens	The pancreas makes little if any insulin.	The pancreas doesn't produce enough insulin or the body doesn't respond properly to the insulin that is produced.
Risk Factors	Less well-defined, but autoimmune, genetic, and environmental factors are believed to be involved.	Older age, obesity, family history of diabetes, physical inactivity, and race/ethnicity.
Treatment	Individualized meal plans, insulin therapy (usually several injections a day), self-monitoring glucose testing several times a day, regular physical activity, and a healthy diet.	A healthy diet, weight loss (if overweight), regular exercise, and monitoring blood glucose levels. Some people are able to manage blood sugar through diet and exercise alone. However, diabetes tends to be a progressive disease, so oral medications and possibly insulin may be needed at some point.

Foods to Eat

Vegetables

Fresh vegetables never cause harm to anyone. So, adding a meal full of vegetables is the best shot for all diabetic patients. But not all vegetables contain the same number of macronutrients. Some vegetables contain a high amount of carbohydrates, so those are not suitable for a diabetic diet. We need to use vegetables which contain a low amount of carbohydrates.

1. Cauliflower
2. Spinach
3. Tomatoes
4. Broccoli
5. Lemons
6. Artichoke
7. Garlic
8. Asparagus
9. Spring onions
10. Onions
11. Ginger, etc.

Meat

Meat is not on the red list for the diabetic diet. It is fine to have some meat every now and then for diabetic patients. However certain meat types are better than others. For instance, red meat is not a preferable option for such patients. They should consume white meat more often whether it's seafood or poultry. Healthy options in meat are:

1. All fish, i.e., salmon, halibut, trout, cod, sardine, etc.
2. Scallops
3. Mussels
4. Shrimp
5. Oysters, etc.

Fruits

Not all fruits are good for diabetes. To know if the fruit is suitable for this diet, it is important to note its sugar content. Some fruits contain a high number of sugars in the form of sucrose and fructose, and those should be readily avoided. Here is the list of popularly used fruits that can be taken on the diabetic diet:

1. Peaches
2. Nectarines
3. Avocados
4. Apples
5. Berries
6. Grapefruit
7. Kiwi Fruit
8. Bananas
9. Cherries
10. Grapes
11. Orange
12. Pears
13. Plums
14. Strawberries

Nuts and Seeds

Nuts and seeds are perhaps the most enriched edibles, and they contain such a mix of macronutrients that can never harm anyone. So diabetic patients can take the nuts and seeds in their diet without any fear of a glucose spike.

1. Pistachios
2. Sunflower seeds
3. Walnuts
4. Peanuts
5. Pecans
6. Pumpkin seeds
7. Almonds
8. Sesame seeds, etc.

Grains

Diabetic patients should also be selective while choosing the right grains for their diet. The idea is to keep the amount of starch as minimum as possible. That is why you won't see any white rice in the list rather it is replaced with more fibrous brown rice.

1. Quinoa
2. Oats
3. Multigrain
4. Whole grains
5. Brown rice
6. Millet
7. Barley

8. Sorghum
9. Tapioca

Fats

Fat intake is the most debated topic as far as the diabetic diet is concerned. As there are diets like ketogenic, which are loaded with fats and still proved effective for diabetic patients. The key is the absence of carbohydrates. In any other situation, fats are as harmful to diabetics as any normal person. Switching to unsaturated fats is a better option.

1. Sesame oil
2. Olive oil
3. Canola oil
4. Grapeseed oil
5. Other vegetable oils
6. Fats extracted from plant sources

Diary

Any dairy product which directly or indirectly causes a glucose rise in the blood should not be taken on this diet. Other than those, all products are good to use. These items include:

1. Skimmed milk
2. Low-fat cheese
3. Eggs
4. Yogurt
5. Trans fat-free margarine or butter

Sugar Alternatives

Since ordinary sugars or sweeteners are strictly forbidden on a diabetic diet. There are artificial varieties that can add sweetness without raising the level of carbohydrates in the meal. These substitutes are:

1. Stevia
2. Xylitol
3. Natvia
4. Swerve
5. Monk fruit
6. Erythritol

Make sure to substitute them with extra care. The sweetness of each sweetener is entirely different from the table sugar, so add each in accordance with the intensity of their flavor. Stevia is the sweetest of them, and it should be used with more care. In place of 1 c of sugar, 1 tsp of stevia is enough. All other sweeteners are more or less similar to sugar in their intensity of sweetness.

Foods to Avoid

Knowing a general scheme of diet helps a lot, but it is equally important to be well familiar with the items which have to be avoided. With this list, you can make your diet 100 % sugar-free. There are many other food items that can cause some harm to a diabetic patient as the sugars do. So, let's discuss them in some detail here.

Sugars

Sugar is a big NO-GO for a diabetic diet. Once you are diabetic, you would need to say goodbye to all the natural sweeteners which are loaded with carbohydrates. They contain polysaccharides that readily break into glucose after getting into our body. And the list does not only include table sugars but other items like honey and molasses should also be avoided.

1. White sugar
2. Brown sugar
3. Confectionary sugar
4. Honey
5. Molasses
6. Granulated sugar

Your mind and your body, will not accept the abrupt change. It is recommended to go for a gradual change. It means start substituting it with low carb substitutes in a small amount, day by day.

High Fat Dairy Products

Once you are diabetic, you may get susceptible to a number of other fatal diseases including cardiovascular ones. That is why experts strictly recommend avoiding high-fat food products, especially dairy items. The high amount of fat can make your body insulin resistant. So even when you take insulin, it won't be of any use as the body will not work on it.

Saturated Animal Fats

Saturated animal fats are not good for anyone, whether diabetic or normal. So, better avoid using them in general. Whenever you are cooking meat, try to trim off all the excess fat. Cooking oils made out of these saturated fats should be avoided. Keep yourself away from any of the animal-origin fats.

High Carb Vegetables

As discussed above, vegetables with more starch are not suitable for diabetes. These veggies can increase the carbohydrate levels of food. So, omit these from the recipes and enjoy the rest of the less starchy vegetables. Some of the high carb vegetables are:

1. Potatoes
2. Sweet potatoes
3. Yams, etc.

Cholesterol Rich Ingredients

Bad cholesterol or high-density lipoprotein has the tendency to deposit in different parts of the body. That is why food items having high bad cholesterol are not good for diabetes. Such items should be replaced with the ones with low cholesterol.

High Sodium Products

Sodium is related to hypertension and blood pressure. Since diabetes is already the result of a hormonal imbalance in the body, in the presence of excess sodium—another imbalance—a fluid imbalance may occur which a diabetic body cannot tolerate. It adds up to already present complications of the disease. So, avoid using food items with a high amount of sodium. Mainly store packed items, processed foods, and salt all contain sodium, and one should avoid them all. Use only the unsalted variety of food products, whether it's butter, margarine, nuts, or other items.

Sugary Drinks

Cola drinks or other similar beverages are filled with sugars. If you had seen different video presentations showing the amount of the sugars present in a single bottle of soda, you would know how dangerous those are for diabetic patients. They can drastically increase the amount of blood glucose level within 30 minutes of drinking. Fortunately, there are many sugar-free varieties available in the drinks which are suitable for diabetic patients.

Sugar Syrups and Toppings

A number of syrups available in the markets are made out of nothing but sugar. Maple syrup is one good example. For a diabetic diet, the patient should avoid such sugary syrups and also stay away from the sugar-rich toppings available in the stores. If you want to use them at all, trust yourself and prepare them at home with a sugar-free recipe.

Sweet Chocolate and Candies

For diabetic patients, sugar-free chocolates or candies are the best way out. Other processed chocolate bars and candies are extremely damaging to their health, and all of these should be avoided. You can try and prepare healthy bars and candies at home with sugar-free recipes.

Alcohol

Alcohol has the tendency to reduce the rate of our metabolism and take away our appetite, which can render a diabetic patient into a very life-threatening condition. Alcohol in a very small amount cannot harm the patient, but the regular or constant intake of alcohol is bad for health and glucose levels.

Chapter 2. Breakfast

1. Strawberries Oatmeal

Preparation Time: 5 minutes

Cooking Time: 15 minutes

Servings: 4

- ½ cup coconut shredded
- ¼ cup strawberries
- 2 cups coconut milk
- ¼ tsp. vanilla extract
- 2 tsp. stevia
- Cooking spray

Ingredients:

Directions:

1. Grease the Air Fryer's pan with the cooking spray, add all the ingredients inside, and toss
2. Cook at 365°F for 15 minutes, divide into bowls and serve for breakfast

Nutrition:

- Calories: 142
- Fat: 7g
- Fiber: 2g
- Carbohydrates: 3g
- Protein: 5g

2. Tuna Sandwiches

Preparation Time: 10 minutes

Cooking Time: 5 minutes

Ingredients:

- 16 oz canned tuna, drained
- ¼ cup mayonnaise
- 2 tablespoons mustard
- 1 tablespoon lemon juice
- 2 green onions, chopped
- 3 English muffins, halved

Servings: 2

- 3 tablespoons butter
- 6 provolone cheese

Directions:

1. In a bowl, mix tuna with mayo, lemon juice, mustard, and green onions and stir.
2. Grease muffin halves with the butter, place them in the preheated Air Fryer, and bake them at 350°F for 4 minutes.
3. Spread tuna mix on muffin halves, top each with provolone cheese, return sandwiches to Air Fryer and cook them for 4 minutes, divide among plates and serve for breakfast right away. Enjoy!

Nutrition:

- Calories: 182
- Fat: 4g
- Fiber: 7g
- Carbohydrates: 8g
- Protein: 6g

3. Garlic Potatoes with Bacon

Preparation Time: 10 minutes

Cooking Time: 20 minutes

Servings: 2

- 6 garlic cloves, minced
- 4 bacon slices, chopped
- 2 rosemary springs, chopped
- 1 tablespoon olive oil
- Salt and black pepper to the taste
- 2 eggs, whisked

Ingredients:

- 4 potatoes, peeled and cut into medium cubes

Directions:

1. In your Air Fryer's pan, mix oil with potatoes, garlic, bacon, rosemary, salt, pepper, and eggs and whisk.
2. Cook potatoes at 400 degrees F for 20 minutes, divide everything on plates, and serve for breakfast. Enjoy!

Nutrition:

- Calories: 211
- Fat: 3g
- Fiber: 5g
- Carbohydrates: 8g
- Protein: 5g

4. Chicken & Zucchini Omelet

Preparation Time: 15 minutes

Cooking Time: 35 minutes

Servings: 2

- ½ cup milk
- Salt and ground black pepper to taste
- 1 cup cooked chicken, chopped
- 1 cup Cheddar cheese, shredded
- ½ cup fresh chives, chopped
- ¾ cup zucchini, chopped

Ingredients:

- 8 eggs

Directions:

1. In a bowl, add the eggs, milk, salt, and black pepper and beat well. Add the remaining ingredients and stir to combine. Place the mixture into a greased baking pan. Press the "Power Button" of Air Fry Oven and turn the dial to select the "Air Bake" mode.

2. Press the Time button and again turn the dial to set the cooking time to 35 minutes. Now push the Temp button and rotate the dial to set the temperature at 315 degrees F.
3. Press the "Start/Pause" button to start. When the unit beeps to show that it is preheated, open the lid. Arrange pan over the "Wire Rack" and insert in the oven.
4. Cut into equal-sized wedges and serve hot.

Nutrition:

- Calories: 209
- Fat: 13.3 g
- Carbohydrates: 2.3 g
- Fiber: 0.3 g
- Sugar: 1.8 g
- Protein: 9.8 g

5. Tomatoes and Swiss Chard Bake

Preparation Time: 5 minutes

Cooking Time: 15 minutes

Servings: 4

Ingredients:

- 4 eggs whisked
- 3 oz. Swiss chard chopped.
- 1 cup tomatoes cubed
- 1 tsp. olive oil
- Salt and black pepper to taste.

Directions:

1. Take a bowl and mix the eggs with the rest of the ingredients except the oil and whisk well.
2. Grease a pan that fits the fryer with the oil, pour the Swiss chard mix, and cook at 359°F for 15 minutes.
3. Divide between plates and serve.

Nutrition:

- Calories: 202
- Fat: 14g
- Fiber: 3g
- Carbohydrates: 5g
- Protein: 12g

6. Shrimp Frittata

Cooking Time: 15 minutes

Servings: 2

Preparation Time: 10 minutes

Ingredients:

- 4 eggs
- ½ teaspoon basil, dried
- Cooking spray
- Salt and black pepper to the taste
- ½ cup rice, cooked
- ½ cup shrimp, cooked, peeled, deveined, and chopped
- ½ cup baby spinach, chopped
- ½ cup Monterey jack cheese, grated

Directions:

1. In a bowl, mix eggs with salt, pepper, and basil and whisk. Grease your Air Fryer's pan with cooking spray and add rice, shrimp, and spinach. Add eggs mix, sprinkle cheese all over and cook in your Air Fryer at 350 degrees F for 10 minutes.
2. Divide among plates and serve for breakfast. Enjoy!

Nutrition:

- Calories: 162
- Fat: 6
- Fiber: 5
- Carbohydrates: 8
- Protein: 4

7. Zucchini Fritters

Preparation Time: 15 minutes

Servings: 2

Cooking Time: 7 minutes

Ingredients:

- 10½ oz. zucchini, grated and squeezed
- 7 oz. Halloumi cheese
- ¼ cup all-purpose flour
- 2 eggs
- 1 teaspoon fresh dill, minced
- Salt and ground black pepper, as required

Directions:

1. In a large bowl and mix together all the ingredients.
2. Make a small-sized fritter from the mixture.
3. Press "Power Button" of Air Fry Oven and turn the dial to select the "Air Fry" mode.
4. Press the Time button and again turn the dial to set the cooking time to 7 minutes.
5. Now push the Temp button and rotate the dial to set the temperature at 355°F.
6. Press the "Start/Pause" button to start.
7. When the unit beeps to show that it is preheated, open the lid.
8. Arrange fritters into grease "Sheet Pan" and insert in the oven.
9. Serve warm.

Nutrition:

- Calories: 253
- Fat: 17.2 g
- Carbohydrates: 10 g
- Fiber: 1.1 g
- Sugar: 2.7 g
- Protein: 15.2 g

8. Chicken Omelet

Preparation Time: 10 minutes

Servings: 2

Cooking Time: 16 minutes

Ingredients:

- 1 teaspoon butter
- 1 small yellow onion, chopped
- ½ jalapeño pepper, seeded and chopped
- 3 eggs
- Salt and ground black pepper to taste
- ¼ cup cooked chicken, shredded

Directions:

1. In a frying pan, melt the butter over medium heat and cook the onion for about 4-5 minutes. Add the jalapeño pepper and cook for about 1 minute.

2. Remove from the heat and set aside to cool slightly. Meanwhile, in a bowl, add the eggs, salt, and black pepper and beat well.
3. Add the onion mixture and chicken and stir to combine. Place the chicken mixture into a small baking pan.
4. Press "Power Button" of Air Fry Oven and turn the dial to select the "Air Fry" mode.
5. Press the Time button and again turn the dial to set the cooking time to 6 minutes.
6. Now push the Temp button and rotate the dial to set the temperature at 355°F.
7. Press the "Start/Pause" button to start.
8. When the unit beeps to show that it is preheated, open the lid.
9. Arrange pan over the "Wire Rack" and insert in the oven.
10. Cut the omelet into 2 portions and serve hot.

Nutrition:

- Calories: 153
- Fat: 9.1 g
- Carbohydrates: 4 g
- Fiber: 0.9 g
- Sugar: 2.1 g
- Protein: 13.8 g

9. Scrambled Eggs

Preparation Time: 5 minutes

Cooking Time: 20 minutes

Servings: 2

Ingredients:

- 4 large eggs.
- ½ cup shredded sharp Cheddar cheese.
- 2 tbsp. unsalted butter melted.

Directions:

1. Crack eggs into a 2-cup round baking dish and whisk.
2. Place dish into the Air Fryer basket.
3. Adjust the temperature to 400°F and set the timer for 10 minutes.
4. After 5 minutes, stir the eggs and add the butter and cheese.
5. Let cook for 3 more minutes and stir again.
6. Allow eggs to finish cooking an additional 2 minutes or remove if they are to your desired liking.
7. Use a fork to fluff. Serve warm.

Nutrition:

- Calories: 359
- Protein: 19.5g
- Fiber: 0.0g
- Fat: 27.6g
- Carbohydrates: 1.1g

10. Almond Crust Chicken

Preparation Time: 10 minutes

Cooking Time: 25 minutes

Servings: 2

Ingredients:

- 2 chicken breasts, skinless and boneless
- 1 tbsp Dijon mustard
- 2 tbsp mayonnaise
- ¼ cup almonds
- Pepper to taste

- Salt to taste

Directions:
1. Add almond into the food processor and process until finely ground.
2. Transfer almonds to a plate and set them aside.
3. Mix mustard and mayonnaise and spread over chicken.
4. Coat chicken with almond and place it into the Air Fryer basket and cook at 350°F for 25 minutes.
5. Serve and enjoy.

Nutrition:
- Calories: 409
- Fat: 22 g
- Carbohydrates: 6 g
- Sugar: 1.5 g
- Protein: 45 g

11. Mushroom Cheese Salad

Preparation Time: 10 minutes

Cooking Time: 15 minutes

Ingredients:
- 10 mushrooms, halved
- 1 tbsp. fresh parsley, chopped
- 1 tbsp. olive oil
- 1 tbsp. mozzarella cheese, grated
- 1 tbsp. cheddar cheese, grated
- 1 tbsp. dried mix herbs

Servings: 2
- Pepper to taste
- Salt to taste

Directions:
1. Add all ingredients into the bowl and toss well
2. Transfer bowl mixture into the Air Fryer baking dish
3. Place in the Air Fryer and cook at 380°F for 15 minutes.
4. Serve and enjoy.

Nutrition:
- Calories: 90
- Fat: 7 g
- Carbohydrates: 2 g
- Sugar: 1 g
- Protein: 5 g

12. Shrimp Sandwiches

Preparation Time: 10 minutes

Cooking Time: 5 minutes

Servings: 2

Ingredients:
- 1 and ¼ cups cheddar, shredded
- 6 oz canned tiny shrimp, drained
- 3 tablespoons mayonnaise
- 2 tablespoons green onions, chopped
- 4 whole-wheat bread slices
- 2 tablespoons butter, soft

Directions:

1. In a bowl, mix shrimp with cheese, green onion, and mayo, and stir well. Spread this on half of the bread slices, top with the other bread slices, cut into halves diagonally, and spread butter on top.
2. Place sandwiches in your Air Fryer and cook at 350 degrees F for 5 minutes.
3. Divide shrimp sandwiches and serve them for breakfast. Enjoy!

Nutrition:

- Calories: 162
- Fat: 3g
- Fiber: 7g
- Carbohydrates: 12g
- Protein: 4g

13. Mushrooms and Cheese Spread

Preparation Time: 5 minutes

Cooking Time: 20 minutes

Servings: 4

Ingredients:

- ¼ cup mozzarella shredded
- ½ cup coconut cream
- 1 cup white mushrooms
- A pinch of salt and black pepper
- Cooking spray

Directions:

1. Put the mushrooms in your Air Fryer's basket, grease with cooking spray, and cook at 370°F for 20 minutes.
2. Transfer to a blender, add the remaining ingredients, pulse well, divide into bowls and serve as a spread

Nutrition:

- Calories: 202
- Fat: 12g
- Fiber: 2g
- Carbohydrates: 5g
- Protein: 7g

14. Lemony Raspberries Bowls

Preparation Time: 5 minutes

Cooking Time: 12 minutes

Servings: 2

Ingredients:

- 1 cup raspberries
- 2 tbsp. butter
- 2 tbsp. lemon juice
- 1 tsp. cinnamon powder

Directions:

1. In your Air Fryer, mix all the ingredients, toss, cover, cook at 350°F for 12 minutes, divide into bowls and serve for breakfast

Nutrition:

- Calories: 208
- Fat: 6g
- Fiber: 9g
- Carbohydrates: 14g
- Protein: 3g

15. Asparagus Salad

Preparation Time: 5 minutes

Cooking Time: 10 minutes

Servings: 4

- 1 tbsp. balsamic vinegar
- 1 tbsp. cheddar cheese grated
- A pinch of salt and black pepper
- Cooking spray
- 1 cup baby arugula
- 1 bunch asparagus trimmed

Directions:

1. Put the asparagus in your Air Fryer's basket, grease with cooking spray, season with salt and pepper, and cook at 360°F for 10 minutes.
2. Take a bowl and mix the asparagus with the arugula and the vinegar, toss, divide between plates and serve hot with cheese sprinkled on top

Nutrition:

- Calories: 200
- Fat: 5g
- Fiber: 1g
- Carbohydrates: 4g
- Protein: 5g

16. Zucchini Squash Mix

Preparation Time: 10 minutes

Cooking Time: 35 minutes

Servings: 2

- 1 tbsp parsley, chopped
- 1 yellow squash, halved, deseeded, and chopped
- 1 tbsp olive oil
- Pepper to taste
- Salt to taste

Ingredients:

- 1 lb. zucchini, sliced

Directions:

1. Add all ingredients into the large bowl and mix well.
2. Transfer bowl mixture into the Air Fryer basket and cook at 400°F for 35 minutes.
3. Serve and enjoy.

Nutrition:

- Calories: 49
- Fat: 3 g
- Carbohydrates: 4 g
- Sugar: 2 g
- Protein: 1.5 g

17. Bacon-Wrapped Filet Mignon

Preparation Time: 10 minutes

Cooking Time: 15 minutes

Servings: 2

Ingredients:

- 2 bacon slices
- 2 (4-ounce) filet mignon
- Salt and ground black pepper, as required
- Olive oil cooking spray

Directions:

1. Wrap 1 bacon slice around each filet mignon and secure with toothpicks.
2. Season the fillets with salt and black pepper lightly.
3. Arrange the filet mignon onto a cooling rack and spray with cooking spray.
4. Arrange the drip pan in the bottom of the Air Fryer Oven cooking chamber.
5. Select "Air Fry" and then adjust the temperature to 375 degrees F.
6. Set the timer for 15 minutes and press the "Start".
7. When the display shows "Add Food" insert the cooking rack in the center position.
8. When the display shows "Turn Food" turn the filets.
9. When cooking time is complete, remove the rack from Air Fryer oven and serve hot.

Nutrition:

- Calories: 360
- Fat: 19.6 g
- Carbohydrates: 0.4 g
- Protein: 42.6 g

18. Pumpkin Pancakes

Preparation Time: 15 minutes

Cooking Time: 12 minutes

Servings: 2

Ingredients:

- 1 square puff pastry
- 3 tablespoons pumpkin filling n
- 1 small egg, beaten

Directions:

1. Roll out a square of puff pastry and layer it with pumpkin pie filling, leaving about ¼-inch space around the edges. Cut it up into 8 equal-sized square pieces and coat the edges with a beaten egg.
2. Press "Power Button" of Air Fry Oven and turn the dial to select the "Air Fry" mode. Press the Time button and again turn the dial to set the cooking time to 12 minutes. Now push the Temp button and rotate the dial to set the temperature at 355 degrees F. Press the "Start/Pause" button to start.
3. When the unit beeps to show that it is preheated, open the lid. Arrange the squares into a greased sheet pan and insert them in the oven. Serve warm.

Nutrition:

- Calories: 109
- Fat: 6.7 g
- Carbohydrates: 9.8 g
- Fiber: 0.5 g
- Sugar: 2.6 g
- Protein: 2.4 g

19. Onion Omelet

Preparation Time: 10 minutes

Cooking Time: 15 minutes

Servings: 2

Ingredients:

- 4 eggs
- ¼ teaspoon low-sodium soy sauce
- Ground black pepper, as required
- 1 teaspoon butter
- 1 medium yellow onion, sliced
- ¼ cup Cheddar cheese, grated

Directions:

1. In a skillet, melt the butter over medium heat and cook the onion and cook for about 8-10 minutes.
2. Remove from the heat and set aside to cool slightly.
3. Meanwhile, in a bowl, add the eggs, soy sauce, and black pepper and beat well.
4. Add the cooked onion and gently, stir to combine.
5. Place the zucchini mixture into a small baking pan. Press "Power Button" of Air Fry Oven and turn the dial to select the "Air Fry" mode.
6. Press the Time button and again turn the dial to set the cooking time to 5 minutes.
7. Now push the Temp button and rotate the dial to set the temperature at 355 degrees F. Press the "Start/Pause" button to start.
8. When the unit beeps to show that it is preheated, open the lid.
9. Arrange the pan over the "Wire Rack" and insert it in the oven.
10. Cut the omelet into 2 portions and serve hot.

Nutrition:

- Calories: 222
- Carbohydrates: 6.1 g
- Fiber: 1.2 g
- Sugar: 3.1 g
- Protein: 15.3 g

20. Sweetened Breakfast Oats

Preparation Time: 10 minutes

Cooking Time: 7 minutes

Servings: 4

Ingredients:

- 1 cup steel-cut oats
- 3/4 cup shredded coconut
- 1/4 tsp ground ginger
- 1/4 tsp ground nutmeg
- 1/2 tsp ground cinnamon
- 1/4 cup raisins
- 1 large apple, chopped
- 2 large carrots, grated

- 1 cup of coconut milk
- 3 cups of water

Directions:

1. Add oats, nutmeg, ginger, cinnamon, raisins, apple, carrots, milk, and water into the instant pot and stir to combine.
2. Seal pot with lid and cook on manual mode for 4 minutes.
3. Once done then allow to release pressure naturally for 20 minutes then release using the quick-release method. Open the lid.
4. Top with coconut and serve.

Nutrition:

- Calories: 341
- Fat: 20.8 g
- Carbohydrates: 38.2 g
- Sugar: 16.1 g
- Protein: 5.3 g

Chapter 3. Recipes for Lunch

21. Easy Rosemary Lamb Chops

Preparation Time: 10 minutes

Cooking Time: 6 minutes

Servings: 4

- 4 lamb chops
- 2 tbsps. dried rosemary
- ¼ cup fresh lemon juice
- Pepper to taste
- Salt to taste

Ingredients:

-

Directions:

1. In a medium bowl, mix lemon juice, rosemary, pepper, and salt. Brush lemon juice rosemary mixture over lamb chops.
2. Place lamb chops on Air Fryer oven tray and air fry at 400°F for 3 minutes. Turn lamb chops to the other side and cook for 3 minutes more. Serve and enjoy.

Nutrition:

- Calories: 267
- Fat: 21.7 g.
- Carbohydrates 1.4 g.
- Protein: 16.9 g.

22. Greek Lamb Chops

Preparation Time: 10 minutes

Cooking Time: 10 minutes

Servings: 4

- 2 tsps. garlic, minced
- 1 ½ tsp. dried oregano
- ¼ cup fresh lemon juice
- ¼ cup olive oil
- ½ tsp. pepper
- 1 tsp. salt

Ingredients:

- 2 lbs. lamb chops

Directions:

1. Add lamb chops in a mixing bowl. Add the remaining ingredients over the lamb chops and coat well.
2. Arrange lamb chops on the Air Fryer oven tray and cook at 400°F for 5 minutes.
3. Turn lamb chops and cook for 5 minutes more.

4. Serve and enjoy.

Nutrition:

- Calories: 538
- Fat: 29.4 g.
- Carbohydrates 1.3 g.
- Protein: 64 g.

23. Easy Beef Roast

Preparation Time: 10 minutes

Cooking Time: 45 minutes

Servings: 6

Ingredients:

- 2 ½ lbs. beef roast
- 2 tbsps. Italian seasoning

Directions:

1. Arrange roast on the rotisserie spite.
2. Rub roast with Italian seasoning then insert into the Instant Vortex Air Fryer Oven.
3. Air fry at 350°F for 45 minutes or until the internal temperature of the roast reaches 145°F.
4. Slice and serve.

Nutrition:

- Calories: 365
- Fat: 13.2 g.
- Carbohydrates 0.5 g.
- Protein: 57.4 g.

24. Juicy Pork Chops

Preparation Time: 10 minutes

Cooking Time: 16 minutes

Servings: 4

Ingredients:

- 4 pork chops, boneless
- 2 tsps. olive oil
- ½ tsp. celery seed
- ½ tsp. parsley
- ½ tsp. granulated onion
- ½ tsp. granulated garlic
- ¼ tsp. sugar
- ½ tsp. salt

Directions:

1. In a small bowl, mix oil, celery seed, parsley, granulated onion, granulated garlic, sugar, and salt.
2. Rub seasoning mixture all over the pork chops.
3. Place pork chops on the Air Fryer oven pan and cook at 350°F for 8 minutes.
4. Turn pork chops to the other side and cook for 8 minutes more.
5. Serve and enjoy.

Nutrition:

- Calories: 279
- Fat: 22.3 g.
- Carbohydrates 0.6 g.
- Protein: 18.1 g.

25. Tuna and Spring Onions Salad

Preparation Time: 5 minutes

Cooking Time: 15 minutes

Servings: 4

Ingredients:

- 14 oz. canned tuna, drained and flaked
- 2 spring onions chopped
- 1 cup arugula
- 1 tbsp. olive oil
- A pinch of salt and black pepper

Directions:

1. In a media bowl, add all ingredients except the oil and arugula and whisk.
2. Preheat the Air Fryer over 360°F, add oil, and grease it. Pour the tuna mix, stir well and cook for 15 minutes.
3. In a salad bowl, combine the arugula with the tuna mix, toss and serve.

Nutrition:

- Calories: 212
- Fat: 8 g.
- Fiber: 3 g.
- Carbohydrates: 5 g.
- Protein: 8 g.

26. Bacon-Wrapped Filet Mignon

Preparation Time: 10 minutes

Cooking Time: 15 minutes

Ingredients:

- 2 bacon slices
- 2 (4 oz.) fillet mignon
- Salt and ground black pepper, as required

Servings: 2

- Olive oil cooking spray mignon

Directions:

1. Wrap 1 bacon slice around each fillet and secure with toothpicks.
2. Season the fillets with salt and black pepper lightly.
3. Arrange the fillet mignon onto a cooking rack and spray with cooking spray.
4. Place the drip pan in the cooking chamber of the Instant Vortex Plus Air Fryer Oven.
5. Choose "Air Fry" and set the temperature to 375°F.
6. Press the "Start" button after setting the timer for 15 minutes.
7. Place the frying rack in the center position when the display says "Add Food."
8. When the display shows "Turn Food" turn the fillets.
9. When cooking time is complete, remove the rack from Vortex and serve hot.

Nutrition:

- Calories: 360
- Fat: 19.6 g.
- Carbohydrates 0.4 g.
- Protein: 42.6 g.

27. Classic Beef Jerky

Preparation Time: 10 minutes

Cooking Time: 4 hours

Servings: 4

Ingredients:

- 2 lbs. London broil, sliced thinly
- 1 tsp. onion powder
- 3 tbsps. brown sugar
- 3 tbsps. soy sauce
- 1 tsp. olive oil
- ¾ tsp. garlic powder

Directions:

1. Add all ingredients except meat in the large zip-lock bag.
2. Mix until well combined. Add meat to the bag.
3. Seal bag and massage gently to cover the meat with marinade.
4. Let marinate the meat for 1 hour.
5. Arrange marinated meat slices on an Instant Vortex Air Fryer Tray and dehydrate at 160°F for 4 hours.

Nutrition:

- Calories: 133
- Fat: 4.7 g.
- Carbohydrates 9.4 g.
- Protein: 13.4 g.

28. Flavorful Steak

Preparation Time: 10 minutes

Cooking Time: 18 minutes

Servings: 2

Ingredients:

- 2 steaks, rinsed and pat dry
- ½ tsp. garlic powder
- 1 tsp. olive oil
- Pepper to taste
- Salt to taste

Directions:

1. Rub steaks with olive oil and season with garlic powder, pepper, and salt.
2. Preheat the Instant Vortex Air Fryer Oven to 400°F.
3. Place steaks on Air Fryer oven pan and air fry for 10–18 minutes turning halfway through.
4. Serve and enjoy.

Nutrition:

- Calories: 361
- Fat: 10.9 g.
- Carbohydrates 0.5 g.
- Protein: 61.6 g.

29. BBQ Pork Chops

Preparation Time: 10 minutes

Cooking Time: 7 minutes

Servings: 4

Ingredients:

- 4 pork chops

For the rub:

- ½ tsp. allspice
- ½ tsp. dry mustard
- 1 tsp. ground cumin
- 1 tsp. garlic powder
- ½ tsp. chili powder
- ½ tsp. paprika
- 1 tbsp. brown sugar
- 1 tsp. salt

Directions:

1. In a small bowl, mix all rub ingredients and rub all over pork chops.
2. Arrange pork chops on Air Fryer tray and air fry at 400°F for 5 minutes.
3. Turn pork chops to the other side and air fry for 2 minutes more.
4. Serve and enjoy.

Nutrition:

- Calories: 273
- Fat: 20.2 g.
- Carbohydrates 3.4 g.
- Protein: 18.4 g.

30. 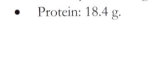 Crispy Meatballs

Preparation Time: 10 minutes

Cooking Time: 12 minutes

Ingredients:

- 1 lb. ground pork
- 1 lb. ground beef
- 1 tbsp. Worcestershire sauce
- ½ cup feta cheese, crumbled
- ½ cup breadcrumbs
- 2 eggs, lightly beaten
- ¼ cup fresh parsley, chopped
- 1 tbsp. garlic, minced

- 1 tsp. salt

Servings: 8

- 1 onion, chopped
- ¼ tsp. pepper

Directions:

1. Add all ingredients into the mixing bowl and mix until well combined.
2. Spray Air Fryer oven tray pan with cooking spray.
3. Make small balls from the meat mixture and arrange them on a pan and air fry at 400°F for 10–12 minutes.
4. Serve and enjoy.

Nutrition:

- Calories: 263
- Fat: 9 g.
- Carbohydrates 7.5 g.
- Protein: 35.9 g.

31. Juicy Steak Bites

Preparation Time: 10 minutes

Cooking Time: 9 minutes

Servings: 4

- 1 lb. sirloin steak, cut into bite-size pieces
- 1 tbsp. steak seasoning
- 1 tbsp. olive oil
- Pepper to taste
- Salt to taste

Ingredients:

Directions:

1. Preheat the Instant Vortex Air Fryer Oven to 390°F.
2. Add steak pieces into the large mixing bowl. Add steak seasoning, oil, pepper, and salt over steak pieces and toss until well coated.
3. Transfer steak pieces on instant vortex Air Fryer pan and air fry for 5 minutes.
4. Turn steak pieces to the other side and cook for 4 minutes more.
5. Serve and enjoy.

Nutrition:

- Calories: 241
- Fat: 10.6 g.
- Carbohydrates 0 g.
- Protein: 34.4 g.

32. Lemon Garlic Lamb Chops

Preparation Time: 10 minutes

Cooking Time: 6 minutes

Servings: 6

- 2 tbsps. fresh lemon juice
- 1 ½ tbsp. lemon zest
- 1 tbsp. dried rosemary
- 1 tbsp. olive oil
- 1 tbsp. garlic, minced
- Pepper to taste
- Salt to taste

Ingredients:

- 6 lamb loin chops

Directions:

1. Add lamb chops in a mixing bowl. Add the remaining ingredients on top of lamb chops and coat well.
2. Arrange lamb chops on Air Fryer oven tray and air fry at 400°F for 3 minutes. Turn lamb chops to another side and air fry for 3 minutes more. Serve and enjoy.

Nutrition:

- Calories: 69
- Fat: 6 g.

- Carbohydrates 1.2 g.
- Protein: 3 g.

33. BBQ Pork Ribs

Preparation Time: 10 minutes

Cooking Time: 12 minutes

Servings: 6

Ingredients:

- 1 slab baby back pork ribs, cut into pieces
- ½ cup BBQ sauce
- ½ tsp. paprika
- Salt to taste

Directions:

1. Add pork ribs to a mixing bowl. Add BBQ sauce, paprika, and salt over pork ribs and coat well, and set aside for 30 minutes.
2. Preheat the Instant Vortex Air Fryer Oven to 350°F.
3. Arrange marinated pork ribs on Instant Vortex Air Fryer Oven pan and cook for 10–12 minutes. Turn halfway through.
4. Serve and enjoy.

Nutrition:

- Calories: 145
- Fat: 7 g.
- Carbohydrates 10 g.
- Protein: 9 g.

34. Herb Butter Rib-Eye Steak

Preparation Time: 10 minutes

Cooking Time: 14 minutes

Servings: 4

Ingredients:

- 2 lbs. rib eye steak, bone-in
- 1 tsp. fresh rosemary, chopped
- 1 tsp. fresh thyme, chopped
- 1 tsp. fresh chives, chopped
- 2 tsp. fresh parsley, chopped
- 1 tsp. garlic, minced
- ¼ cup butter softened
- Pepper to taste
- Salt to taste

Directions:

1. In a small bowl, combine butter and herbs.
2. Refrigerate the rib-eye steak for 30 minutes after rubbing it with herb butter.
3. Place the marinated steak on an Instant Vortex Air Fryer Oven pan and cook for 12–14 minutes at 400°F.
4. Serve and enjoy.

Nutrition:

- Calories: 416
- Fat: 36.7 g.
- Carbohydrates 0.7 g.
- Protein: 20.3 g.

35. Honey Mustard Pork Tenderloin

Preparation Time: 10 minutes

Cooking Time: 26 minutes

Servings: 4

- 1 tsp. sriracha sauce
- 1 tbsp. garlic, minced
- 2 tbsps. soy sauce
- 1 ½ tbsp. honey
- ¾ tbsp. Dijon mustard
- 1 tbsp. mustard

Ingredients:

- 1 lb. pork tenderloin

Directions:

1. Add sriracha sauce, garlic, soy sauce, honey, Dijon mustard, and mustard into the large zip-lock bag and mix well.
2. Add pork tenderloin into the bag. Seal bag and place in the fridge overnight. Preheat the Instant Vortex Air Fryer Oven to 380°F.
3. Spray Instant Vortex Air Fryer Tray with cooking spray then place marinated pork tenderloin on a tray and air fry for 26 minutes.
4. Turn pork tenderloin after every 5 minutes.
5. Slice and serve.

Nutrition:

- Calories: 195
- Fat: 4.1 g.
- Carbohydrates 8 g.
- Protein: 30.5 g.

36. Simple Beef Sirloin Roast

Preparation Time: 10 minutes

Cooking Time: 50 minutes

Servings: 8

Ingredients:

- 2 ½ lbs. sirloin roast
- Salt and ground black pepper, as required
-

Directions:

1. Season the roast well with salt and black pepper.
2. Through the roast, insert the rotisserie rod.
3. To secure the rod to the bird, place one rotisserie fork on each side of the rod.
4. Place the drip pan in the cooking chamber of the Instant Vortex Plus Air Fryer Oven.
5. Select "Roast" and set the temperature to 350°F.
6. Press the "Start" button after setting the timer for 50 minutes.
7. Press the red lever down and load the left side of the rod into the Vortex when the display says "Add Food."

8. Now, slide the rod's left side into the metal bar's groove to keep it from moving. Then close the door and press the "Rotate" button. When the cooking time is up, press the red lever to release the rod.
9. Remove the roast from the Vortex and set it aside for 10 minutes before slicing. Cut the roast into desired-sized slices with a sharp knife and serve.

Nutrition:

- Calories: 201
- Fat: 8.8 g.
- Carbohydrates 0 g.
- Protein: 28.9 g.

37. Seasoned Beef Roast

Preparation Time: 10 minutes

Cooking Time: 45 minutes

Servings: 10

Ingredients:

- 3 lbs. beef top roast
- 1 tbsp. olive oil
- 2 tbsps. Montreal steak seasoning

Directions:

1. Coat the roast with oil and then rub with the seasoning generously.
2. With kitchen twines, tie the roast to keep it compact. Arrange the roast onto the cooking tray.
3. Place the drip pan in the cooking chamber of the Instant Vortex Plus Air Fryer Oven.
4. Choose "Air Fry" and set the temperature to 360°F. Press the "Start" button after you set the timer for 45 minutes.
5. Place the cooking tray in the center position when the display says "Add Food."
6. Do nothing when the display says "Turn Food."
7. Remove the tray from the Vortex when the cooking time is up and set the roast on a platter for about 10 minutes before slicing. Cut the roast into desired-sized slices with a sharp knife and serve.

Nutrition:

- Calories: 259
- Fat: 9.9 g.
- Carbohydrates 0 g.
- Fiber: 0 g.

38. Beef Burgers

Preparation Time: 15 minutes

Cooking Time: 18 minutes

Servings: 4

Ingredients:

For the burgers:

- 1 lb. ground beef
- ½ cup panko breadcrumbs

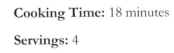

- ¼ cup onion, chopped finely
- 3 tbsps. Dijon mustard
- 3 tsps. low-sodium soy sauce
- 2 tsps. fresh rosemary, chopped finely
- Salt, to taste

For the topping:

- 2 tbsps. Dijon mustard
- 1 tbsp. brown sugar

- 1 tsp. soy sauce
- 4 Gruyere cheese slices

Directions:

1. In a large bowl, add all ingredients and mix until well combined.
2. Make 4 equal-sized patties from the mixture.
3. Arrange the patties onto a cooking tray.
4. Arrange the drip pan in the bottom of the Instant Vortex Plus Air Fryer Oven cooking chamber.
5. Select "Air Fry" and then adjust the temperature to 370°F.
6. Set the timer for 15 minutes and press the "Start."
7. When the display shows "Add Food" insert the cooking rack in the center position.
8. When the display shows "Turn Food" turn the burgers.
9. Meanwhile, make the sauce by mixing the mustard, brown sugar, and soy sauce in a small basin.
10. Remove the tray from the Vortex after the cooking time is up and coat the burgers in the sauce.
11. 1 slice of cheese on top of each burger
12. Select "Broil" when returning the tray to the cooking chamber.
13. Press the "Start" button after setting the timer for 3 minutes.
14. Remove the dish from the Vortex after the cooking time is up and serve hot.

Nutrition:

- Calories: 412
- Fat: 18 g.
- Carbohydrates 6.3 g.
- Protein: 44.4 g.

39. Season and Salt-Cured Beef

Preparation Time: 15 minutes

Cooking Time: 3 hours

Servings: 4

Ingredients:

- 1 ½ lb. beef round, trimmed
- ½ cup Worcestershire sauce
- ½ cup low-sodium soy sauce
- 2 tsps. honey
- 1 tsp. liquid smoke
- 2 tsps. onion powder
- ½ tsp. red pepper flakes
- Ground black pepper, as required

Directions:

1. In a bag zip-top, place the beef and freeze for 1–2 hours to firm up.
2. Place the meat onto a cutting board and cut against the grain into 1/8–¼-inch strips.
3. In a large bowl, add the remaining ingredients and mix until well combined.
4. Add the steak slices and coat with the mixture generously.
5. Refrigerate to marinate for about 4–6 hours.
6. Remove the beef slices from the bowl and with paper towels, pat dry them.
7. Arrange the steak pieces in an equal layer on the baking trays.
8. Choose "Dehydrate" and set the temperature to 160°F.
9. Press the "Start" button after setting the timer for 3 hours.
10. Insert one tray in the top position and the other in the center position when the display says "Add Food."
11. Switch the position of the cooking trays after 1–2 hours.
12. Meanwhile, boil the remaining ingredients in a small saucepan over medium heat for about 10 minutes, stirring regularly.
13. Remove the trays from the Vortex after the cooking time is finished.

Nutrition:

- Calories: 362
- Fat: 10.7 g.
- Carbohydrates 11 g.
- Protein: 53.8 g.

40. Simple Beef Patties

Preparation Time: 10 minutes

Cooking Time: 13 minutes

Servings: 4

Ingredients:

- 1 lb. ground beef
- ½ tsp. garlic powder
- ¼ tsp. onion powder
- Pepper
- Salt

Directions:

1. Preheat the Instant Vortex Air Fryer Oven to 400°F.
2. Add ground meat, garlic powder, onion powder, pepper, and salt into the mixing bowl and mix until well combined.
3. Make even shape patties from the meat mixture and arrange them on the Air Fryer pan.
4. Place pan in instant vortex Air Fryer oven.
5. Cook patties for 10 minutes Turn patties after 5 minutes
6. Serve and enjoy.

Nutrition:

- Calories: 212
- Fat: 7.1 g.
- Carbohydrates 0.4 g.
- Protein: 34.5 g.

Chapter 4. Recipes for Dinner

41. Brine-Soaked Turkey

Preparation Time: 10 minutes

Cooking Time: 45 minutes

Servings: 8

3 cloves garlic, smashed
5 sprigs of fresh thyme
3 bay leaves
Black pepper

Ingredients:

7 lb. bone-in, skin-on turkey breast

For the brine:

½ cup salt
1 lemon
½ onion

For the turkey breast:

4 tbsps. butter, softened
½ tsp. black pepper
½ tsp. garlic powder
¼ tsp. dried thyme
¼ tsp. dried oregano

Directions:

Mix the turkey brine ingredients in a pot and soak the turkey in the brine overnight. The next day, remove the soaked turkey from the brine.

Whisk the butter, black pepper, garlic powder, oregano, and thyme. Brush the butter mixture over the turkey then places it in a baking tray.

To select the "Air Roast" mode, press the "Power Button" on the Air Fry Oven and spin the dial. To set the cooking time to 45 minutes, press the "Time" button and then turn the dial again.

To set the temperature, press the "Temp" button and rotate the dial to 370°F. Place the turkey baking pan in the oven and close the cover once it has been preheated.

Slice and serve warm.

Nutrition:

Calories: 397
Fat: 15.4 g.
Carbohydrates 58.5 g.
Protein: 7.9 g.

42. Oregano Chicken Breast

Preparation Time: 10 minutes

Cooking Time: 25 minutes

Ingredients:

2 lbs. chicken breasts, minced
1 tbsp. avocado oil
1 tsp. smoked paprika

Servings: 6

1 tsp. garlic powder
1 tsp. oregano
½ tsp. salt
Black pepper, to taste

Directions:

Toss all the meatball ingredients in a bowl and mix well. Make small meatballs out of this mixture and place them in the Air Fryer basket.
Press the "Power Button" of Air Fry Oven and turn the dial to select the "Air Fry" mode. Press the "Time" button and again turn the dial to set the cooking time to 25 minutes
Now push the "Temp" button and rotate the dial to set the temperature at 375°F.
Once preheated, place the Air Fryer basket inside and close its lid.
Serve warm.

Nutrition:

Calories: 352
Fat: 14 g
Carbohydrates: 15.8 g
Protein: 26 g

43. Thyme Turkey Breast

Ingredients:

Preparation Time: 10 minutes

Cooking Time: 40 minutes

Servings: 4

2 lbs. turkey breast
Salt, to taste
Black pepper, to taste
4 tbsps. butter, melted
3 cloves garlic, minced
1 tsp. thyme, chopped
1 tsp. rosemary, chopped

Directions:

Mix butter with salt, black pepper, garlic, thyme, and rosemary in a bowl.
Rub this seasoning over the turkey breast liberally and place it in the Air Fryer basket.
Turn the dial to select the "Air Fry" mode.
Hit the "Time" button and again use the dial to set the cooking time to 40 minutes.
Now push the "Temp" button and rotate the dial to set the temperature at 375°F.
Once preheated, place the Air Fryer basket inside the oven.
Slice and serve fresh.

Nutrition:

Calories: 334
Fat: 4.7 g.
Carbohydrates 54.1 g.
Protein: 26.2 g.

44. Chicken Drumsticks

Preparation Time: 10 minutes

Cooking Time: 20 minutes

Ingredients:

8 chicken drumsticks
2 tbsps. olive oil
1 tsp. salt

Servings: 8

1 tsp. pepper
1 tsp. garlic powder
1 tsp. paprika
½ tsp. cumin

Directions:

Mix olive oil with salt, black pepper, garlic powder, paprika, and cumin in a bowl.
Rub this mixture liberally over all the drumsticks.
Place these drumsticks in the Air Fryer basket.
Turn the dial to select the "Air Fry" mode.
Hit the "Time" button and again use the dial to set the cooking time to 20 minutes.
Now push the "Temp" button and rotate the dial to set the temperature at 375°F.
Once preheated, place the Air Fryer basket inside the oven.
Flip the drumsticks when cooked halfway through.
Resume air frying for another rest of the 10 minutes.
Serve warm.

Nutrition:

Calories: 212
Fat: 11.8 g.
Carbohydrates: 14.6 g.
Protein: 17.3 g.

45. Lemon Chicken Breasts

Preparation Time: 10 minutes

Cooking Time: 30 minutes

Servings: 4

4 boneless skin-on chicken breasts
1 sliced lemon
1 tbsp. grated lemon zest
2 tbsps. lemon juice
1 ½ tbsp. crushed dried oregano
1 tsp. chopped thyme leaves
black pepper and salt to taste
¼ cup extra virgin olive oil
3 tsps. minced garlic

Ingredients:

1/3 cup white wine, dry

Directions:

In a baking pan, whisk together all ingredients to thoroughly coat the chicken breasts.
Serve the chicken breasts with lemon wedges on top.
Over the toasted bread slices, spread the mustard mixture.
To select the "Bake" mode, press the "Power Button" on the Air Fry Oven and spin the dial.
To set the cooking time to 30 minutes, press the "Time" button and then turn the dial again.
To set the temperature, press the "Temp" button and rotate the dial to 370°F.
Place the baking pan inside and close the lid once the oven has been warmed.
Warm the dish before serving.

Nutrition:

Calories: 388
Fat: 8 g.
Carbohydrates: 8 g.
Protein: 13 g.

46. Parmesan Chicken Meatballs

Preparation Time: 10 minutes

Cooking Time: 12 minutes

Servings: 4

Ingredients:

- 1 lb. ground chicken
- 1 large egg, beaten
- ½ cup Parmesan cheese, grated
- ½ cup pork rinds, ground
- 1 tsp. garlic powder
- 1 tsp. paprika
- 1 tsp. kosher salt
- ½ tsp. pepper

For the crust:

- ½ cup pork rinds, ground

Directions:

Toss all the meatball ingredients in a bowl and mix well. Make small meatballs out of this mixture and roll them in the pork rinds.

Place the coated meatballs in the Air Fryer basket. Select "Power Button" of Air Fry Oven and turn the control to select the "Bake" mode.

Press the "Time" button and again turn the control to set the cooking time to 12 minutes. Now push the "Temp" button and rotate the dial to set the temperature at 400°F.

Once preheated, place the Air Fryer basket inside and close its lid.

Serve warm.

Nutrition:

Calories: 529
Fat: 17 g.
Carbohydrates: 55 g.
Protein: 41 g.

47. Easy Italian Meatballs

Preparation Time: 10 minutes

Cooking Time: 13 minutes

Servings: 4

Ingredients:

- 2 lbs. lean ground turkey
- ¼ cup onion, minced
- 2 cloves garlic, minced
- 2 tbsps. parsley, chopped
- 2 eggs
- 1 ½ cup parmesan cheese, grated
- ½ tsp. red pepper flakes
- ½ tsp. Italian seasoning
- Salt and black pepper to taste

Directions:

Toss all the meatball ingredients in a bowl and mix well. Make small meatballs out of this mixture and place them in the Air Fryer basket.

Select the "Air Fry" mode by pressing the "Power Button" on the Air Fry Oven and turning the dial. To set the cooking time to 13 minutes, press the "Time" button and then turn the dial again. To set the temperature, press the "Temp" button and crank the dial to 350°F.

Once preheated, place the Air Fryer basket inside and close its lid.

Flip the meatballs when cooked halfway through.

Serve warm.

Nutrition:

Calories: 472
Fat: 25.8
Carbohydrates: 1.7 g.
Protein: 59.6 g.

48. Buttered Salmon

Preparation Time: 5 minutes

Cooking Time: 10 minutes

Servings: 2

Ingredients:

- 2 (6 oz.) salmon fillets
- Salt and ground black pepper, as required
- 1 tbsp. butter, melted

Directions:

Season each salmon fillet with salt and black pepper and then, coat with the butter. Arrange the salmon fillets onto the greased cooking tray.

Arrange the drip pan in the bottom of the Instant Vortex Air Fryer Oven cooking chamber. Select "Air Fry" and then adjust the temperature to 360°F. Set the time for 10 minutes and press "Start."

When the display shows "Add Food" insert the cooking tray in the center position. When the display shows "Turn Food" turn the salmon fillets.

When cooking time is complete, remove the tray from the Vortex Oven. Serve hot.

Nutrition:

Calories: 276
Carbohydrates: 0 g.
Fat: 16.3 g.
Protein: 33.1 g.

49. Crispy Haddock

Preparation Time: 5 minutes

Cooking Time: 10 minutes

Servings: 3

Ingredients:

- ½ cup flour
- ½ tsp. paprika
- 1 egg, beaten
- ¼ cup mayonnaise
- 4 oz. salt and vinegar potato chips, crushed finely
- 1 lb. haddock fillet cut into 6 pieces

Directions:

In a shallow dish, mix the flour and paprika. In a second shallow dish, add the egg and mayonnaise and beat well. In a third shallow dish, place the crushed potato chips.

Coat the fish pieces with flour mixture, then dip into the egg mixture, and finally coat with the potato chips. Arrange the fish pieces onto 2 cooking trays.

Place the drip pan in the cooking chamber of the Instant Vortex Air Fryer Oven. Select "Air Fry" and set the temperature to 370°F. Set the timer for 10 minutes and hit the "Start" button.

Insert one cooking tray in the top position and another in the bottom position when the display says "Add Food."

When the display says "Turn Food," don't turn the food instead, move the cooking trays around. Remove the trays from the Vortex Oven when the cooking time is up. Serve immediately.

Nutrition:

Calories: 456
Carbohydrates: 40.9 g.
Fat: 22.7 g.
Protein: 43.5 g.

50. Miso Glazed Salmon

Preparation Time: 5 minutes

Cooking Time: 10 minutes

Servings: 4

Ingredients:

1/3 cups sake
¼ cups sugar
¼ cups red miso
1 tbsp. low-sodium soy sauce
2 tbsps. vegetable oil
4 (5 oz.) skinless salmon fillets, 1-inch thick

Directions:

Place's sake, sugar, miso, soy sauce, and oil into a bowl and beat until thoroughly combined. Rub the salmon fillets with the mixture generously. In a plastic zip-lock bag, place the salmon fillets with any remaining miso mixture.

Seal the bag and refrigerate to marinate for about 30 minutes Grease a baking dish that will fit in the Vortex Air Fryer Oven. Remove the salmon fillets from the bag and shake off the excess marinade. Arrange the salmon fillets into the prepared baking dish.

Place the drip pan in the bottom of the Instant Vortex Air Fryer Oven cooking chamber. Select "Broil" and set the time for 5 minutes.

When the display shows "Add Food" insert the baking dish in the center position.

When the display shows "Turn Food" do not turn the food. When cooking time is complete, remove the baking dish from the Vortex Oven. Serve hot.

Nutrition:

Calories: 335
Carbohydrates: 18.3 g.
Fat: 16.6 g.
Protein: 29.8 g.

51. Ground Chicken Meatballs

Preparation Time: 10 minutes

Cooking Time: 10 minutes

Servings: 4

Ingredients:

1 lb. ground chicken
1/3 cup panko
1 tsp. salt
2 tsps. chives
½ tsp. garlic powder
1 tsp. thyme
1 egg

Directions:

Toss all the meatball ingredients in a bowl and mix well. Make small meatballs out of this mixture and place them in the Air Fryer basket.

Press the "Power Button" of Air Fry Oven and turn the dial to select the "Air Fry" mode. Press the "Time" button and again turn the dial to set the cooking time to 10 minutes.

Now push the "Temp" button and rotate the dial to set the temperature at 350°F. Once preheated, place the Air Fryer basket inside and close its lid. Serve warm.

Nutrition:

Calories: 453
Fat: 2.4 g.
Carbohydrates: 18 g.
Protein: 23.2 g.

52. Lemony Salmon

Preparation Time: 5 minutes

Cooking Time: 10 minutes

Servings: 2

Ingredients:

1 tbsp. fresh lemon juice
½ tbsp. olive oil
Salt and ground black pepper, as required
1 garlic clove, minced
½ tsp. fresh thyme leaves, chopped

2 (7 oz.) salmon fillets

Directions:

Combine all ingredients in a mixing dish, except the salmon, and stir thoroughly. Add the salmon fillets and generously cover them in the mixture.

Place the salmon fillets skin-side down on a lightly greased frying rack. Place the drip pan in the cooking chamber of the Instant Vortex Air Fryer Oven. Select "Air Fry" and set the temperature to 400°F. Set the timer for 10 minutes and hit the "Start" button.

Place the frying rack in the bottom position when the display says "Add Food." Turn the fillets when the display says "Turn Food."

Remove the tray from the Vortex Oven after the cooking time is over. Serve immediately.

Nutrition:

Calories: 297
Carbohydrates: 0.8 g.
Fat: 15.8 g.
Protein: 38.7 g.

53. Crispy Tilapia

Preparation Time: 5 minutes

Cooking Time: 15 minutes

Servings: 2

Ingredients:

¾ cup cornflakes, crushed
1 (1 oz.) packet dry ranch-style dressing mix
2 ½ tbsps. vegetable oil
2 eggs

4 (6 oz.) tilapia fillets

Directions:

In a shallow bowl, beat the eggs. In another bowl, add the cornflakes, ranch dressing, and oil and mix until a crumbly mixture forms. Dip the fish fillets into the egg and then, coat with the cornflake mixture.

Arrange the tilapia fillets onto the greased cooking tray. Arrange the drip pan in the bottom of the Instant Vortex Air Fryer Oven cooking chamber. Select "Air Fry" and then adjust the temperature to 355°F. Set the time for 14 minutes and press "Start."

When the display shows "Add Food" insert the cooking tray in the center position. When the display shows "Turn Food" turn the tilapia fillets. When cooking time is complete, remove the tray from the Vortex Oven. Serve hot.

Nutrition:

Calories: 291
Carbohydrates: 4.9 g.
Fat: 14.6 g.
Protein: 34.8 g.

54. Vinegar Halibut

Preparation Time: 5 minutes

Cooking Time: 12 minutes

Servings: 2

Ingredients:

2 (5 oz.) halibut fillets
1 garlic clove, minced
1 tsp. fresh rosemary, minced

1 tbsp. olive oil
1 tbsp. red wine vinegar
1/8 tsp. hot sauce

Directions:

In a large resealable bag, add all ingredients. Seal the bag and shale well to mix. Refrigerate to marinate for at least 30 minutes. Remove the fish fillets from the bag and shake off the excess marinade. Arrange the halibut fillets onto the greased cooking tray.

Place the drip pan in the cooking chamber of the Instant Vortex Air Fryer Oven. Select "Bake" and set the temperature to 450°F. Set the timer for 12 minutes and hit the "Start" button. Place the cooking tray in the center position when the display says "Add Food." Turn the halibut fillets when the display says "Turn Food." Remove the tray from the Vortex Oven after the cooking time is over. Serve immediately.

Nutrition:

Calories: 223
Carbohydrates: 1 g.
Fat: 10.4 g.
Protein: 30 g.

55. Crusted Chicken Drumsticks

Preparation Time: 10 minutes

Cooking Time: 10 minutes

Servings: 4

Ingredients:

1 lb. chicken drumsticks
½ cup buttermilk
½ cup panko breadcrumbs
½ cup flour
¼ tsp. baking powder

For the spice mixture:

½ tsp. salt
½ tsp. celery salt
¼ tsp. oregano
¼ tsp. cayenne
1 tsp. paprika
¼ tsp. garlic powder
¼ tsp. dried thyme
½ tsp. ground ginger
½ tsp. white pepper

½ tsp. black pepper

3 tbsps. butter melted

Directions:

Soak chicken in the buttermilk and cover to marinate overnight in the refrigerator. Mix spices with flour, breadcrumbs, and baking powder in a shallow tray.
Remove the chicken from the milk and coat them well with the flour spice mixture.
Place the chicken drumsticks in the Air Fryer basket of the Ninja Oven.
Pour the melted butter over the drumsticks.
Turn the dial to select the "Air Fry" mode. Hit the "Time" button and again use the dial to set the cooking time to 10 minutes.
Now push the "Temp" button and rotate the dial to set the temperature at 425°F.
Once preheated, place the baking tray inside the oven.
Flip the drumsticks and resume cooking for another 10 minutes.
9 Serve warm.

Nutrition:

Calories: 331
Fat: 2.5 g.
Carbohydrates: 69 g.
Protein: 28.7 g.

56. Spiced Tilapia

Preparation Time: 5 minutes

Servings: 2

Cooking Time: 12 minutes

Ingredients:

½ tsp. lemon-pepper seasoning
½ tsp. garlic powder
½ tsp. onion powder

Salt and ground black pepper, as required
2 (6 oz.) tilapia fillets
1 tbsp. olive oil

Directions:

In a small bowl, mix the spices, salt, and black pepper. Coat the tilapia fillets with oil and then rub with spice mixture. Arrange the tilapia fillets onto a lightly greased cooking rack, skin-side down.
Arrange the drip pan in the bottom of the Instant Vortex Air Fryer Oven cooking chamber. Select "Air Fry" and then adjust the temperature to 360°F. Set the time for 12 minutes and press "Start."
Place the frying rack in the lowest position when the display says "Add Food." Turn the fillets when the display says "Turn Food."
When the time of cooking is complete, remove the tray from the Vortex Oven. Serve hot.

Nutrition:

Calories: 206
Carbohydrates: 0.2 g.
Fat: 8.6 g.
Protein: 31.9 g.

57. Simple Haddock

Preparation Time: 5 minutes

Servings: 2

Cooking Time: 10 minutes

Ingredients:

2 (6 oz.) haddock fillets

1 tbsp. olive oil
Salt and ground black pepper, as required

Directions:

Coat the haddock fillets with oil and then, sprinkle with salt and black pepper. Arrange the haddock fillets onto a greased cooking rack and spray with cooking spray.

Place the drip pan in the bottom of the Instant Vortex Air Fryer Oven cooking chamber. Select "Air Fry" and then adjust the temperature to 355°F. Set the time for 8 minutes and press "Start."

When the display shows "Add Food" insert the cooking rack in the center position.

When the display shows "Turn Food" do not turn the food.

When the cooking time is complete, remove the rack from the Vortex Oven. Serve hot.

Nutrition:

Calories: 251
Carbohydrates: 0 g.
Fat: 8.6 g.
Protein: 41.2 g.

58. Breaded Cod

Preparation Time: 5 minutes

Cooking Time: 10 minutes

Servings: 4

Ingredients:

- 1/3 cup all-purpose flour
- Ground black pepper, as required
- 1 large egg
- 2 tbsps. water
- 2/3 cup cornflakes, crushed
- 1 tbsp. parmesan cheese, grated
- 1/8 tsp. cayenne pepper
- 1 lb. cod fillets
- Salt, as required

Directions:

In a shallow dish, add the flour and black pepper and mix well. In a second shallow dish, add the egg and water and beat well. In a third shallow dish, add the cornflakes, cheese, and cayenne pepper and mix well.

Season the cod fillets with salt evenly. Coat the fillets with flour mixture, then dip into the egg mixture and finally coat with the cornflake mixture.

Arrange the cod fillets onto the greased cooking rack. Arrange the drip pan in the bottom of the Instant Vortex Air Fryer Oven cooking chamber. Select "Air Fry" and then adjust the temperature to 400°F. Set the time for 15 minutes and press "Start."

Place the frying rack in the lowest position when the display says "Add Food." Turn the fish fillets when the display says "Turn Food." Remove the tray from the Vortex Oven after the cooking time is over. Serve immediately.

Nutrition:

Calories: 168
Carbohydrates: 12.1 g.
Fat: 2.7 g.
Protein: 23.7 g.

59. Spicy Catfish

Preparation Time: 5 minutes

Cooking Time: 15 minutes

Servings: 4

Ingredients:

- 2 tbsps. cornmeal polenta
- 2 tsp. Cajun seasoning
- ½ tsp. paprika
- ½ tsp. garlic powder
- Salt, as required
- 2 (6 oz.) catfish fillets
- 1 tbsp. olive oil

Directions:

In a bowl, mix cornmeal, Cajun seasoning, paprika, garlic powder, and salt. Add catfish fillets and coat evenly with the mixture. Now, coat each fillet with oil.

Arrange the fish fillets onto a greased cooking rack and spray with cooking spray. Place the drip pan in the bottom of the Instant Vortex Air Fryer Oven cooking chamber. Select "Air Fry" and then adjust the temperature to 400°F. Set the timer for 14 minutes and press "Start."

When the display shows "Add Food" insert the cooking rack in the center position. When the display shows "Turn Food" turn the fillets.

When cooking time is complete, remove the rack from the Vortex Oven. Serve hot.

Nutrition:

Calories: 32
Carbohydrates: 6.7 g.
Fat: 20.3 g.
Protein: 27.3 g.

60. Tuna Burgers

Preparation Time: 5 minutes

Cooking Time: 6 minutes

Servings: 4

Ingredients:

7 oz. canned tuna
1 large egg
¼ cup breadcrumbs
1 tbsp. mustard
¼ tsp. garlic powder
¼ tsp. onion powder
¼ tsp. cayenne pepper
Salt and ground black pepper, as required

Directions:

1 In a mixing bowl, combine all ingredients and stir until well blended. Form the ingredients into four equal-sized patties.
2 Place the patties on a prepared baking sheet. Place the drip pan in the cooking chamber of the Instant Vortex Air Fryer Oven. Select "Air Fry" and set the temperature to 400°F. Set the timer for 6 minutes and hit the "Start" button.
3 Place the frying rack in the center position when the display says "Add Food."
4 Turn the burgers when the display says "Turn Food."
5 Remove the tray from the Vortex Oven after the cooking time is over. Serve immediately.

Nutrition:

Calories: 151
Carbohydrates: 6.3 g.
Fat: 6.4 g.
Protein: 16.4 g.

Chapter 5. Vegetarian Recipes

61. Delicious Air Fryer Cauliflower

Preparation Time: 5 minutes

Cooking Time: 10 minutes

Servings: 6

Ingredients:

1/2 tsp fresh lemon juice
3 cups cauliflower
Salt and pepper to taste (very little)
1 tbsp fresh parsley, chopped
¾ tsp dried oregano
1 1/2 tsp olive oil
1 tbsp pine nuts (unsalted)

Directions:

Place the cauliflower in a container and sprinkle it with olive oil. Add oregano, salt, and pepper. Place in the fryer at 375°F and fry for 10 minutes.
Drop into a serving dish and include pine nuts, fresh parsley, and lemon juice.

Nutrition:

Calories: 104
Fat: 7 g
Carbohydrates: 9 g
Protein: 44 g

62. Spinach Quiche

Preparation Time: 10 minutes

Cooking Time: 18/22 minutes

Servings: 3

Ingredients:

3 eggs
1 cup frozen chopped spinach, thawed and drained
1/3 cup heavy cream
2 tablespoons honey mustard
1/2 cup grated Swiss or Havarti cheese
1/2 teaspoon dried thyme

Pinch salt (very little)
Freshly ground black pepper, to taste (very little)
Nonstick baking spray with flour

Directions:

In a medium bowl, beat the eggs until blended. Add the spinach, cream, honey mustard, cheese, thyme, salt and pepper and mix evenly.
Spray a fryer basket or fryer-friendly pan with nonstick spray. Pour the egg mixture inside.
Cook for 18-22 minutes in the Air Fryer at 380°F or until the egg mixture is puffed, lightly golden and set.
Let cool for 5 minutes, then cut into wedges to serve.

Nutrition:

Calories: 203
Total Fat: 15 g
Carbohydrates: 6 g
Protein: 71 g

63. Yellow Squash Fritters

Preparation Time: 15 minutes

Cooking Time: 7/9 minutes

Servings: 4

Ingredients:

1 (3-ounce) package cream cheese, softened
1 egg, beaten
1/2 teaspoon dried oregano
Pinch salt (very little)
Freshly ground black pepper, to taste (very little)
1 medium yellow summer squash, grated
1/3 cup grated carrot
2/3 cup bread crumbs
2 tablespoons olive oil

Directions:

In a medium bowl, combine and mix well the cream cheese with the egg, oregano, salt, and pepper. Add the pumpkin and the carrot and mix well. Add the breadcrumbs and mix well.
Form about 2 tablespoons of this mixture into a patty about 1/2 inch thick. Repeat with the remaining mixture. Brush pancakes with olive oil.
Air-fry until crisp and golden at 380°F, about 7 to 9 minutes.

Nutrition:

Calories: 134
Total Fat: 17 g
Carbohydrates: 16 g
Protein: 56 g

64. Eggplant Parmigiana

Preparation Time: 15 minutes

Cooking Time: 20 minutes

Servings: 4

1 cup chickpea flour
1 tablespoon dried basil
1 tablespoon dried oregano
2 teaspoons garlic granules
2 teaspoons onion granules
1/2 teaspoon sea salt
1/2 teaspoon freshly ground black pepper
Cooking oil spray (sunflower or safflower)
Vegan marinara sauce, to taste (your choice)
Shredded cheese, to taste (preferably mozzarella)

Ingredients:

1 medium eggplant (about 1-pound), sliced into 1/2-inch-thick rounds
2 tablespoons tamari or shoyu
3 tablespoons non-dairy milk, plain and unsweetened

Directions:

Place the eggplant slices in a large bowl, and pour the tamari and milk over the top. Turn the pieces over to coat them as evenly as possible with the liquids. Set aside.

In a medium bowl, combine the flour, basil, oregano, garlic, onion, salt, and pepper and stir well. Set aside.

Spray the Air Fryer basket with oil and set it aside.

Stir the eggplant slices again and transfer them to a plate (stacking is fine). Do not discard the liquid in the bowl.

Bread the eggplant by tossing an eggplant round in the flour mixture. Then, dip in the liquid again. Double up on the coating by placing the eggplant again in the flour mixture, making sure that all sides are nicely breaded. Place in the Air Fryer basket.

Repeat with enough eggplant rounds to make a (mostly) single layer in the Air Fryer basket. (You'll need to cook it in batches so that you don't have too much overlap and it cooks perfectly.)

Spray the tops of the eggplant with enough oil so that you no longer see dry patches in the coating. Fry for 8 minutes at 385°F. Remove the Air Fryer basket and spray the tops again. Turn each piece over, again taking care not to overlap the rounds too much. Spray the tops with oil, again making sure that no dry patches remain. Fry for another 8 minutes, or until nicely browned and crisp.

Repeat until all eggplant is crisp and golden brown.

Finally, place half of the eggplant in a 6-inch round baking dish, 2 inches deep, and cover with the marinara sauce and a sprinkling of vegan cheese. Fry for 3 minutes, or until the sauce is hot and the cheese is melted (be careful not to overcook, or the edges of the eggplant will burn). Serve immediately, plain or over pasta.

Nutrition:

Calories: 217
Total fat: 9 g
Carbohydrates: 38 g
Protein: 69 g

65. Air Fryer Brussels Sprouts

Preparation Time: 10 minutes

Cooking Time: 8/12 minutes

Servings: 2

Ingredients:

1 cup brussels sprouts
1/4 cup balsamic vinegar
3 tbsp. extra-virgin olive oil
Kosher salt to taste (very little)
Freshly ground black pepper to taste (very little)

Directions:

Remove hard ends of Brussels sprouts and discard damaged outer leaves. Rinse under cold water and pat dry. If your sprouts are large, cut them in half. Add and season with oil, salt and pepper.

Arrange the Brussels sprouts in a single layer in the Air Fryer and work in batches if they don't all fit. Bake for 8-12 minutes at 190°C and shake the pan halfway through to brown them evenly. They're ready when they're lightly browned and crispy at the edges.

Serve the sprouts warm, optionally with a balsamic reduction and parmesan cheese.

Nutrition:

Calories: 164
Protein: 69.58 g

Fat: 15.97 g

Carbohydrates: 16.97 g

66. Endives with Bacon Mix

Preparation Time: 15 minutes

Cooking Time: 10 minutes

Ingredients:

4 endives, trimmed and halved
Salt and black pepper to taste (very little)
1 tbsp. olive oil
2 tbsp. bacon, cooked and crumbled
1/2 tsp. nutmeg, ground

Servings: 1

Directions:

Place the endives in your Air Fryer's basket, then add the salt and pepper to taste as well as oil and nutmeg ensure to toss gently.
Cook at a temperature of 360°F for 10 minutes.
Cut the endives into different plates, then sprinkle the bacon as toppings, and serve.

Nutrition:

Calories: 151
Fat: 6
Carbohydrates: 14
Protein: 66

67. Creamy Potatoes

Preparation Time: 10 minutes

Cooking Time: 20 minutes

Servings: 1

Ingredients:

¾ pound potatoes, peeled and cubed
1 tablespoon olive oil
Salt and black pepper, to taste (very little)
1/2 cup Greek yogurt

Directions:

Place potatoes in a bowl, pour water to cover, and leave aside for 10 minutes.
Drain, pat dry, and then transfer to another bowl.
Add salt, pepper, and half of the oil to the potatoes and mix.
Put potatoes in the Air Fryer basket and cook at 360°F for 20 minutes.
In a bowl, mix yogurt with salt, pepper, and the rest of the oil and whisk.
Divide potatoes onto plates, drizzle with yogurt dressing, mix, and serve.

Nutrition:

Calories: 170
Fat: 3 g
Carbohydrates: 20 g
Protein: 75 g

68. Creamy Cabbage

Preparation Time: 10 minutes

Cooking Time: 20 minutes

Ingredients:

- 1/2 green cabbage head, chopped
- 1/2 yellow onion, chopped
- Salt and black pepper, to taste (very little)
- 1/2 cup whipped cream
- 1 tablespoon cornstarch

Servings: 1

Directions:

Put cabbage and onion in the Air Fryer.
In a bowl, mix cornstarch with cream, salt, and pepper. Stir and pour over cabbage.
Mix well and then bake at 400°F for 20 minutes.
Serve.

Nutrition:

Calories: 208
Fat: 10 g
Carbohydrates: 16 g
Protein: 55 g

69. Asparagus & Parmesan

Preparation Time: 10 minutes

Cooking Time: 6 minutes

Servings: 1

- 1 teaspoon sesame oil
- 11 oz asparagus
- 1 teaspoon chicken stock
- 1/2 teaspoon ground white pepper
- 3 oz Parmesan

Ingredients:

Directions:

Wash the asparagus and chop it roughly.
Sprinkle the chopped asparagus with the chicken stock and ground white pepper.
Then sprinkle the asparagus with the sesame oil and shake them.
Place the asparagus in the Air Fryer basket.
Cook them for 4 minutes at 400°F.
Meanwhile, shred Parmesan cheese.
When the time is over shaking the asparagus gently and sprinkle with the shredded cheese.
Cook the asparagus for 2 minutes more at 400°F.
After this, transfer the cooked asparagus to the serving plates.

Nutrition:

Calories: 139
Fat: 11.6 g
Carbohydrates: 7.9 g

Protein: 57.2 g

70. Walnut & Cheese Filled Mushrooms

Preparation Time: 5 minutes

Cooking Time: 10 minutes

Servings: 1

Ingredients:

4 large Portobello mushroom caps
1/3 cup walnuts, minced
1 tbsp canola oil
1/2 cup mozzarella cheese, shredded
1 tbsp fresh parsley, chopped
Cooking Spray

Directions:

Preheat the Air Fryer to 350°F. Grease the Air Fryer basket with cooking spray.
Rub the mushrooms with canola oil and fill them with mozzarella cheese. Top with minced walnuts and arrange on the bottom of the greased Air Fryer basket.
Bake for 10 minutes to 350°F or until golden on top. Remove, let cool for a few minutes and sprinkle with freshly chopped parsley to serve.

Nutrition:

Calories: 110
Carbohydrates: 6 g
Fat: 5 g
Protein: 78 g

71. Chard with Cheddar

Preparation Time: 10 minutes

Cooking Time: 11 minutes

Servings: 1

Ingredients:

3 oz Cheddar cheese, grated
10 oz Swiss chard
3 tablespoons cream
1 tablespoon sesame oil
Salt and pepper to taste (very little)

Directions:

Wash Swiss chard carefully and chop it roughly.
Sprinkle the chopped chard with salt and ground pepper.
Stir it carefully.
Sprinkle Swiss chard with the sesame oil and stir it carefully with the help of 2 spatulas.
Preheat the Air Fryer to 260°F.
Put chopped Swiss chard in the Air Fryer basket and cook for 6 minutes.
Shake it after 3 minutes of cooking.
Then pour the cream into the Air Fryer basket and mix it up.
Cook for 3 minutes more.
Then increase the temperature to 400°F.
Sprinkle with the grated cheese and bake for another 2 minutes.
After this, transfer the meal to the serving plates. Enjoy!

Nutrition:

Calories: 172
Fat: 22.3 g
Carbohydrates: 6.7 g
Protein: 63.3 g

72. Herbed Tomatoes

Preparation Time: 10 minutes

Cooking Time: 15 minutes

Servings: 1

Ingredients:

- 2 big tomatoes, halved and insides scooped out
- Salt and black pepper, to taste (very little)
- 1/2 tablespoon olive oil
- 1 garlic clove, minced
- 1/4 teaspoon thyme, chopped

Directions:

In the Air Fryer, mix tomatoes with thyme, garlic, oil, salt, and pepper.
Mix and cook at 390°F for 15 minutes.
Serve.

Nutrition:

Calories: 112
Fat: 1 g
Carbohydrates: 4 g
Protein: 34 g

73. Spiced Almonds

Preparation Time: 5 minutes

Cooking Time: 12 minutes

Servings: 1

Ingredients:

- 1/2 tsp ground cinnamon
- 1 cup almonds
- 1 egg white
- Sea salt to taste (very little)
- Cooking Spray

Directions:

Preheat the Air Fryer to 310°F.
Grease the Air Fryer basket with cooking spray.
Take a bowl and split the egg whites of the eggs, being careful of the egg skin chips and removing them if necessary.
In another bowl, whisk the egg white with cinnamon and the almonds and mix well to flavor the almonds with the egg white and spices.
Spread the almonds on the bottom of the frying basket and Air-fry for 12 minutes to 310°F, shaking once or twice. Remove and sprinkle with sea salt to serve.

Nutrition:

Calories: 90
Carbohydrates: 3 g
Fat: 2 g
Protein: 45 g

74. Leeks

Preparation Time: 10 minutes

Cooking Time: 7 minutes

Servings: 1

Ingredients:

2 leeks, washed, ends cut, and halved
Salt and black pepper, to taste (very little)

1/2 tablespoon butter, melted
1/2 tablespoon lemon juice

Directions:

Season leeks with melted butter and season with salt and pepper.
Lay it inside the Air Fryer and cook at 350°F for 7 minutes.
Arrange on a platter.
Drizzle with lemon juice and serve.

Nutrition:

Calories: 100
Fat: 4 g
Carbohydrates: 6 g
Protein: 32 g

75. Asparagus

Preparation Time: 5 minutes

Cooking Time: 8 minutes

Servings: 1

Ingredients:

Nutritional yeast, to taste
Olive oil nonstick spray
1 bunch of asparagus

Directions:

Wash asparagus and then trim off thick, woody ends.
Spray asparagus with olive oil spray and sprinkle with yeast.
Add the asparagus to the basket of the Air Fryer in a single layer. Set the temperature to 360°F and set the time to 8 minutes.
Remove them from the fryer and serve.

Nutrition:

Calories: 17
Total Fat: 8 g
Total Carbohydrates: 2 g
Protein: 39 g

76. Lemony Lentils with "Fried" Onions

Preparation Time: 10 minutes

Cooking Time: 30/35 minutes

Servings: 4

Ingredients:

1 cup red lentils
4 cups water
Cooking oil spray (sunflower or safflower)
1 medium-size onion, peeled and cut into 1/4-inch-thick rings
1/2 cup kale, stems removed, thinly sliced
3 large garlic cloves, pressed or minced
2 tablespoons fresh lemon juice
2 teaspoons nutritional yeast
1/2 teaspoon sea salt
1 teaspoon lemon zest
¾ teaspoon freshly ground black pepper

Directions:

In a medium saucepan, place the lentils with the water on the stove and simmer uncovered until the lentils have completely dissolved, about 30 minutes. Stir every 5 minutes or so while cooking so the lentils don't stick to the bottom of the pot.

While the lentils are cooking spray the Air Fryer basket with oil and place the onion rings inside, separating them as much as possible spray them with the oil and sprinkle with a little salt.

Then fry for 5 minutes and remove the Air Fryer basket, stir and spray again with oil.

Fry for another 5 minutes.

All of the onion slices to be crisp and well browned, so if some of the pieces begin to do that, transfer them from the Air Fryer basket to a plate.

Remove the Air Fryer basket and spray the onions again with oil. Fry for another 5 minutes or until all the pieces are crisp and browned.

Add the kale to the hot lentils and stir very well to finish the lentils.

Stir in the garlic, Nutrition yeast, lemon juice, zest, salt, and pepper.

Stir very well, distribute evenly in bowls and top with the crisp onion rings.

Nutrition:

Calories: 120
Total fat: 1 g
Carbohydrates: 39 g
Protein: 85 g

77. Cauliflower Steak

Preparation Time: 12 minutes

Cooking Time: 7 minutes

Servings: 1

Ingredients:

1 medium head cauliflower
1/4 cup blue cheese crumbles
1/4 cup full-fat ranch dressing (not spicy)
1 tbsp. Salted butter melted.

Directions:

Remove cauliflower leaves and slice the head in 1/2-inch-thick slices.

In a small bowl, mix hot sauce with butter and brush the mixture over the cauliflower.

Place each cauliflower steak into the Air Fryer and set the temperature to 400°F. Cook for 7 minutes.

When cooked, edges will begin turning dark and caramelized. Sprinkle steaks with crumbled blue cheese and serve. Drizzle with ranch dressing.

Nutrition:

Calories: 122
Protein: 54.9 g
Fat: 8.4 g
Carbohydrates: 7.7 g

78. Onion Green Beans

Preparation Time: 10 minutes

Cooking Time: 12 minutes

Servings: 1

Ingredients:

11 oz green beans
1 tablespoon onion powder
1 tablespoon olive oil
1/2 teaspoon salt

Directions:

Wash the green beans carefully and place them in the bowl.
Sprinkle the green beans with onion powder, salt, and olive oil.
Shake the green beans carefully.
Preheat the Air Fryer to 400°F.
Put the green beans in the Air Fryer and cook for 8 minutes.
After this, shake the green beans and cook them for 4 minutes more at 400°F.
When the time is over shaking the green beans.
Serve the side dish and enjoy!

Nutrition:

Calories: 175
Fat: 7.2 g
Carbohydrates: 13.9 g
Protein: 63.2 g

79. Green Beans and Cherry Tomatoes

Preparation Time: 10 minutes

Cooking Time: 15 minutes

Servings: 1

Ingredients:

8 oz cherry tomatoes
8 oz green beans
1 tablespoon olive oil
Salt and black pepper, to taste (very little)

Directions:

In a bowl, mix cherry tomatoes with green beans, olive oil, salt, and pepper. Mix.
Cook in the Air Fryer at 400°F for 15 minutes. Shake once.
Serve.

Nutrition:

Calories: 162
Fat: 6 g
Carbohydrates: 8 g
Protein: 89 g

80. Onion Soup

Preparation Time: 5 minutes

Cooking Time: 35 minutes

Servings: 1

Ingredients:

2 large white onions, peeled, sliced

½ cup cubed squash

1 sprig of thyme

1 tbsp. grapeseed oil

2 cups spring water

Extra:

½ teaspoon salt

¼ teaspoon cayenne pepper

Directions:

Take a medium pot, place it over medium heat, add oil, and when hot, add onion and cook for 10 minutes.

Add thyme sprig, switch heat to the low level and then cook onions for 15 to 20 minutes until soft, covering the pan with its lid.

Add the remaining ingredients, stir until mixed and simmer for 5 minutes.

Ladle soup into bowls and then serve.

Nutrition:

Calories: 76
Carbohydrates: 13.1 g
Protein: 2.3 g
Fat: 2.1 g

Chapter 6. Seafood Recipes

81. Grilled Sardines

Preparation Time: 5 minutes

Cooking Time: 20 minutes

Servings: 4

Ingredients:

5 sardines
Herbs of Provence

Directions:

Preheat the Air Fryer to 160°C.
Spray the basket and place your sardines in the basket of your fryer.
Set the timer for 14 minutes. After 7 minutes, remember to turn the sardines so that they are roasted on both sides.

Nutrition:

Calories: 189g
Fat: 10g
Carbohydrates: 0g
Sugars 0g
Protein: 22g

82. Crunchy Air Fryer Fish

Preparation Time: 5 minutes

Cooking Time: 10/15 minutes

Servings: 4

Ingredients:

1/2 cup yellow cornmeal
1/2 tsp garlic powder
1 large egg
1 tsp coarse salt
1/2 tsp black pepper
1 lb. white fish fillets
Lemon and parsley for garnish (Optional)
Oil spray

Directions:

Preheat the Air Fryer for 3 minutes at 400°F.
Beat the egg in a shallow skillet.
In a different deep skillet, mix the cornmeal and spices.
Dry the fish completely.
Drop the fish fillets in the egg allow extra drip into the pan.
Press the fish into the cornmeal combination until well-crusted on the two sides.
Place the coated fish in the basket of the preheated fryer. Spray lightly with oil.
Cook for 10 minutes at 400°F, tossing the fish to ensure uniform cooking.
If there are dry spots, spray a little oil. Take back the basket to the Air Fryer and cook until the fish is well prepared.
Lightly squeeze with lemon and sprinkle with parsley.
Serve immediately.

Nutrition:

Calories: 191
Carbohydrates: 15 g
Protein: 64 g
Fat: 3 g

83. Tuna Zucchini Melts

Preparation Time: 15 minutes

Cooking Time: 7/8 minutes

Servings: 4

Ingredients:

- 4 corn tortillas (unsalted)
- 3 tablespoons softened margarine
- 1 (6-ounce) can chunk light tuna, drained
- 1 cup shredded zucchini, drained by squeezing in a kitchen towel
- 1/3 cup mayonnaise
- 2 tablespoons mustard
- 1 cup parmesan cheese

Directions:

Coat tortillas with softened margarine.
Put in the basket of the Air Fryer and grill for 2 to 3 minutes at 350°F or until the tortillas are crispy
Take out of the basket and set aside.
Combine the tuna, zucchini, mayonnaise, and mustard in a medium bowl and mix well.
Split the tuna mixture between the toasted tortillas. Fold the tortillas together and top each tortilla with a little cheese.
Grill for 2-4 minutes in the Air Fryer at 350°F or until the tuna mixture is hot and cheese is melted and beginning to brown. Serve.

Nutrition:

Calories: 228
Total Fat: 30 g
Carbohydrates: 19 g
Protein: 52 g

84. Buttery Cod

Preparation Time: 5 minutes

Cooking Time: 12/15 minutes

Servings: 4

Ingredients:

- 1 tbsp. parsley, chopped
- 3 tbsp. butter, melted
- 8 cherry tomatoes, halved
- ¼ cup tomato sauce
- 2 cod fillets, cubed

Directions:

Turn on the fryer to 390°F and heat for 2-3 minutes.
Combine butter, cherry tomatoes, tomato sauce, parsley, and cod fillets put them into a pan that works with the air fryer.

Place the pan in the Air Fryer and cook for about 12/15 minutes to 390°F.
After 12 minutes of cooking, divide into four bowls and enjoy.

Nutrition:

Calories: 132
Carbohydrates: 5 g
Protein: 51 g
Fat: 8 g

85. Breaded Coconut Shrimp

Preparation Time: 5 minutes

Cooking Time: 10/15 minutes

Servings: 4

Ingredients:

450 g shrimp
1 cup panko breadcrumbs
1 cup shredded coconut
2 eggs
1/3 cup all-purpose flour

Directions:

Preheat the Air Fryer to 360°Fahrenheit for 3-4 minutes.
Peel and devein the shrimp.
Pour the flour into a bowl.
In another bowl, beat the eggs, and in a third bowl, combine the breadcrumbs and coconut.
Dip the cleaned shrimp into the flour, eggs, and finish with the coconut mixture.
Lightly spray the fryer basket and bake for 10-15 minutes to 360°Fahrenheit or until golden brown.

Nutrition:

Calories: 185
Fat: 12.8 g
Carbohydrates: 3.7 g
Protein: 38.1 g

86. Codfish Nuggets

Preparation Time: 5 minutes

Cooking Time: 20 minutes

Ingredients:

450 g Cod fillet
3 eggs
4 tbsp. olive oil
1 cup almond flour
1 cup gluten-free breadcrumbs
Salt, to taste (very little)

Servings: 4

Directions:

Heat the Air Fryer to 390°F.
Slice the cod into nuggets.
Prepare three bowls. Whisk the eggs in one. Combine the salt, oil, and breadcrumbs in another. Sift the

almond flour into the third one.
Cover each of the nuggets with flour, dip in the eggs, and the breadcrumbs.
Arrange the nuggets in the basket and set the timer for 20 minutes and cook at 390°F.
Serve the fish with your favorite dips or sides.

Nutrition:

Calories: 134
Fat: 10 g
Carbohydrates: 8 g
Protein: 62 g

87. Easy Crab Sticks

Preparation Time: 5 minutes

Cooking Time: 10 minutes

Servings: 4

Ingredients:

1 package Crab sticks
Cooking oil spray, as needed

Directions:

Take each of the sticks out of the package and unroll it until the stick is flat.
Arrange them on the Air Fryer basket and lightly spritz using cooking spray. Set the timer for 10 minutes and cook at 385°F.
If you shred the crab meat, you can cut the time in half, but they will also easily fall through the holes in the basket.

Nutrition:

Calories: 185
Fat: 12.8 g
Carbohydrates: 3.7 g
Protein: 58.1 g

88. Fried Catfish

Preparation Time: 5 minutes

Cooking Time: 22/23 minutes

Servings: 4

Ingredients:

1 tbsp. olive oil
1/4 cup seasoned fish fry
4 Catfish fillets

Directions:

Heat the Air Fryer to reach 400°Fahrenheit before fry time.
Rinse the catfish and pat dry using a paper towel.
Dump the seasoning into a sizeable zipper-type bag.
Add the fish and shake to cover each fillet. Spray with a spritz of cooking oil spray and add to the basket.

Set the timer for 10 minutes and cook at 400°Fahrenheit. Flip, and reset the timer for 10 additional minutes. Turn the fish once more and cook for 2-3 minutes.

Once it reaches the desired crispiness, transfer to a plate, and serve.

Nutrition:

Calories: 176
Fat: 9 g
Carbohydrates: 10 g
Protein: 68 g

89. Zucchini with Tuna

Preparation Time: 10 minutes

Cooking Time: 20/30 minutes

Servings: 4

4 medium zucchinis
120 g of tuna in oil (canned) drained
30 g grated cheese
1 cup pine nuts
Salt, pepper to taste (very little)

Ingredients:

Directions:

Cut the zucchini in half laterally and empty it with a small spoon (set aside the pulp that will be used for filling)
Place zucchini in a Bowl.
In a food processor, put the zucchini pulp, drained tuna, pine nuts, and grated cheese. Mix everything until you get a homogeneous and dense mixture.
Fill the zucchini with the mixture.
Set the fryer to 180°CUP
Bake for 20/30 min. depending on the size of the zucchini. Allow cooling before serving

Nutrition:

Calories: 139
Carbohydrates: 10 g
Fat: 29 g
Protein: 53 g

90. Deep-Fried Prawns

Preparation Time: 15 minutes

Cooking Time: 8/10 minutes

Ingredients:

12 prawns
2 eggs

Servings: 6

Flour, to taste
Breadcrumbs, to taste
1 tsp. oil

Directions:

Remove the head of the shrimp and carefully peel off the carapace.
In a bowl place the eggs and beat them, in another bowl the flour and in a third bowl the breadcrumbs.
Pass the prawns first in the flour, then in the beaten egg, and then in the breadcrumbs.
Preheat the Air Fryer for 1 minute at 150°C
Add the prawns and cook for 4 minutes. If the prawns are large, it will be necessary to cook 6 at a time.

Turn the prawns and cook for another 4 minutes.
They should be served with a yogurt or mayonnaise sauce.

Nutrition:

Calories: 189
Fat: 16

Carbohydrates: 22.3 g
Protein: 61.4 g

91. Monkfish with Olives and Capers

Preparation Time: 25 minutes

Cooking Time: 40 minutes

Servings: 4

Ingredients:

1 monkfish
10 cherry tomatoes
50 g olives
5 capers (unsalted)
1/2 tablespoons olive oil

Salt, to taste (very little)

Directions:

Clean the monkfish well under running water and skin it completely using a sharp knife.
Lay a sheet of aluminum foil inside the basket of the Air Fryer and place the clean, skinless monkfish.
Add chopped tomatoes, olives, capers, oil, and salt.
Set the temperature of the Air Fryer to 160°C
Cook the monkfish for about 40 minutes or until we see the fish is cooked through and has become crispy.

Nutrition:

Calories: 204
Fat: 19 g

Carbohydrates: 26 g
Protein: 54 g

92. Salmon with Pistachio Bark

Preparation Time: 10 minutes

Cooking Time: 25/30 minutes

Ingredients:

600 g salmon fillet
50 g pistachios (unsalted)

Servings: 4

Salt to taste (very little)
1/2 tablespoons olive oil

Directions:

Put the parchment paper on the bottom of the Air Fryer basket and place the salmon fillet in it (it can be cooked whole or already divided into four portions).
Cut the pistachios into thick pieces, grease the top of the fish, salt (very little) and cover everything with the pistachios.
Set the fryer to 180°C and bake for 25/30 minutes.

Nutrition:

Calories: 111.7

Fat: 21.8 g
Carbohydrates: 9.4 g

Protein: 64.7 g

93. Easy Prawn Salad

Preparation Time: 10 minutes

Servings: 4

Cooking Time: 6/8 minutes

Ingredients:

- 1/2 pounds king prawns, peeled and deveined
- Coarse sea salt and ground black pepper, to taste (very little)
- 1 tablespoon fresh lemon juice
- 1 cup mayonnaise
- 1 teaspoon Dijon mustard
- 1 tablespoon fresh parsley, roughly chopped
- 1 teaspoon fresh dill, minced
- 1 shallot, chopped
- Spray oil, to taste

Directions:

Toss the prawns with the salt and black pepper in a lightly greased Air Fryer cooking basket.

Cook the shrimp at 400°F for 6/8 minutes, shaking the basket halfway through cooking to turn the shrimp.

Add shrimp to a salad bowl add all remaining ingredients and mix well to season and blend everything together.

Nutrition:

Calories: 241
Fat: 21.2 g
Carbohydrates: 2.3 g
Protein: 54.7 g

94. Fried Fish Fingers

Preparation Time: 10 minutes

Cooking Time: 10 minutes

Ingredients:

- 2 eggs
- 1/42 cup all-purpose flour
- Sea salt and ground black pepper, to taste (very little)
- 1/2 teaspoon onion powder
- 1/4 teaspoon garlic powder
- 1/4 cup plain breadcrumbs
- 1/2 tablespoons olive oil
- 1 pound codfish fillets, slice into pieces

Servings: 4

Directions:

In a bowl, place the eggs and beat with flour and spices.
In a separate bowl, thoroughly combine the breadcrumbs and olive oil.
Stir to combine the breadcrumbs with the oil well.
Now, dip the fish pieces into the flour mixture to coat them
Roll the fish pieces over the breadcrumb mixture until well coated on all sides.
Bake the fish sticks at 400°F for 10 minutes in the Air Fryer, turning them halfway through cooking.

Nutrition:

Calories: 169

Fat: 7.7 g
Carbohydrates: 3.1 g

Protein: 50.6 g

95. Salmon with Mushrooms and Bell Pepper

Preparation Time: 5 minutes

Cooking Time: 10 minutes

Servings: 2

Ingredients:

- ¼ cup oil
- ¼ cup flour, all-purpose
- 1 bell pepper
- 1 onion, chopped
- 1 lb. salmon fillet, sliced
- 4.5 oz mushrooms
- 2 tomatoes,
- 3 garlic cloves
- 1 tsp. soy sauce
- 1 1 tsp. sugar, white)
- Salt and pepper to taste
- 3 drops hot sauce

Directions:

Add oil into the Air Fryer pot.
Mix bell pepper, chicken, mushrooms, tomatoes, onion, soy sauce, garlic, sugar, and hot sauce.
Add salt and pepper with flour.
Cook at 300°F for 15 minutes.
When done, serve and enjoy!

Nutrition:

Calories: 108
Sodium: 52mg
Protein: 110g
Carbohydrates: 8g
Fat: 10g
Potassium: 877mg

96. Cod and Chicken Broth

Preparation Time: 6 minutes

Cooking Time: 5 minutes

Servings: 3

Ingredients:

- ½ cup butter
- 1 onion, chopped
- 1 pack broccoli, frozen
- 2 cans chicken broth
- 1 tbsp. garlic powder
- 1 lb. cod fillets, sliced
- 2/3 cup cornstarch
- 1 cup water

Directions:

Add butter and onion into the Air Fryer pot.
Mix cod, onion, cornstarch, water, garlic powder, broccoli, and chicken broth.
Cook at 300°F 15 minutes.
When ready, serve and enjoy!

Nutrition:

Calories: 155
Sodium: 775mg
Protein: 40g
Carbohydrates: 10g
Fat: 7g
Potassium: 209.8mg

97. Spinach with Tuna Fish

Preparation Time: 4 minutes

Cooking Time: 10 minutes

Servings: 2

Ingredients:

- 2 tbsp. butter
- 1 onion, chopped
- 2 garlic cloves
- 1 tbsp. cumin powder
- 1 tbsp. paprika
- 1 can tuna fish
- 2 tomatoes, chopped
- 2 cups vegetable broth
- 1 small bunch spinach, chopped
- Cilantro for garnishing

Directions:

Add butter into the Air Fryer pot.
Mix tuna fish, onion, garlic, cumin powder, paprika, and vegetable broth.
Add tomatoes and spinach.
Cook at 300°F for 10 minutes.
When ready, enjoy!

Nutrition:

- Calories: 95
- Sodium: 960mg
- Protein: 200g
- Carbohydrates: 10g
- Fat: 6g
- Potassium: 761mg

98. Sweet Potato with Tilapia

Preparation Time: 5 minutes

Cooking Time: 10 minutes

Servings: 2

Ingredients:

- 2 lbs. sweet potatoes, cubes
- 2 garlic cloves
- Salt to taste
- 1 lb. tilapia fillets
- 1 tbsp. sage
- 1 tbsp. rosemary
- 2 tbsp. butter
- 2 cups grated cheese

Directions:

Add garlic cloves into the Air Fryer pot.
Mix sage, butter, and rosemary.
Add sweet potatoes with salt.
Cook at 300°F for 10 minutes.
When ready, enjoy the tasty meal!

Nutrition:

- Calories: 90
- Sodium: 317mg
- Protein: 25g
- Carbohydrates: 20g
- Fat: 8g
- Potassium: 378mg

Chapter 7. Snacks

99. Tacos Crispy Avocado

Preparation Time: 10 minutes

Cooking Time: 10 minutes

Servings: 5

Ingredients:

1 avocado
1/2 cup panko crumbs (65 g)
1 large egg whisked
1/4 cup all-purpose flour (35 g)
4 flour tortillas
Pinch each salt and pepper

Adobo Sauce:

1/4 tsp lime juice
1/4 cup plain yogurt (60 g)
1 tbsp. Adobo sauce from a jar of chipotle peppers
2 tbsp. Mayonnaise (30 g)
Polte peppers

Salsa:

1 garlic clove, minced
1 Roma tomato, finely chopped
1 cup pineapple, finely chopped
1/2 red bell pepper, finely chopped
1/2 of a medium red onion
Pinch each cumin and salt
½ not spicy jalapeno, finely chopped

Avocado tacos:

Directions:

- Sauce: mix all sauce ingredients together and refrigerate.
- Prepare avocado: halve the length of the avocado, remove the stone and place the avocado skin face down cut each half into 4 equal pieces. Then gently peel off the skin.
- Prep station: heat t Air Fryer to 190°C Arrange your work area so you have a bowl of flour, a bowl of whisked egg, a bowl of Panko with S & P, and a baking sheet lined with baking paper at the end.
- Coating: dip each avocado slice in flour, egg, and then panko. Place on the prepared baking sheet and fry in the Air Fryer for 10 minutes at 190°C
- Sauce: While cooking avocados, mix all sauce ingredients together.
- Place salsa on a tortilla and add 2 pieces of avocado. Drizzle with salsa and serve immediately.

Nutrition:

Calories: 93
Protein: 53.7 g
Fat: 13.25 g
Carbohydrates: 4.69 g

100. Apple Chips With Cinnamon and Yogurt Sauce

Preparation Time: 5 minutes

Cooking Time: 12 minutes

Servings: 4

Ingredients:

230 g apple (such as Fuji or Honeycrisp)
1 tsp. ground cinnamon
2 tsp. canola oil
Cooking oil spray (as needed)

1/4 cup plain 1% low-fat Greek yogurt
1 tsp. honey

1 tbsp. almond butter

Directions:

Heat the fryer unit to reach 375°F/191°Celsius.
Thinly slice the apple on a mandoline. Toss the slices in a bowl with cinnamon and canola oil to evenly cover.
Spritz the fryer basket using cooking spray.
Arrange seven to eight sliced apples in the basket (single-layered).
Air-fry them for 12 minutes at 375°F (flipping them every 4 min.), and rearrange slices to flatten them. They will continue to crisp upon cooling. Continue the procedure with the rest of the apple slices.
Whisk the yogurt with the almond butter and honey in a mixing container until smooth.
Arrange six to eight sliced apples on each plate with a small dollop of dipping sauce.

Nutrition:

Carbohydrates: 17 g
Fat: 3 g
Protein: 58 g
Calories: 104

101. Mozzarella Cheese Bites with Marinara Sauce

Preparation Time: 15 minutes

Cooking Time: 1 hour + 6/10 minutes

Servings: 12 cheese bites or 6 servings

Ingredients:

1 egg, lightly beaten
1 tbsp. water
1/2 cup all-purpose flour
1/2 tbsp. salt
1/2 tsp. dried Italian seasoning
3/4 cup panko breadcrumbs

6 Mozzarella cheese sticks
Cooking spray
3/4 cup marinara sauce
Red Pepper, to taste (very little)

Directions:

Slice the mozzarella cheese sticks in half—crosswise.
Whisk egg with water in a shallow mixing dish.
Stir the flour with salt and Italian seasoning in another shallow dish.
Place breadcrumbs in a third shallow dish.
Dip the cheese sticks into the egg mixture, then cover using the flour mixture. Dredge again into the egg mix, then into breadcrumbs until coated.
Arrange them on a baking tray—freeze until firm (1 hr.).
Preheat the Air Fryer to reach 360°Fahrenheit/182°Celsius.
Lightly coat the fryer basket using a spritz of cooking spray.
Place frozen cheese bites in the Air Fryer (single-layered), working in batches if necessary, being careful not to crowd.
Cook in the preheated Air Fryer until golden brown and cheese just begins to melt (4-6 min.). Repeat with the rest of the bites.
Meanwhile, whisk the marinara sauce and red pepper to your liking.
Serve the bites with marinara sauce.

Nutrition:

Carbohydrates: 22.6 g
Fat Content: 6.7 g
Protein: 50.9 g
Calories: 122.9

102. Spanakopita Bites

Preparation Time: 10 minutes

Cooking Time: 12 minutes

Servings: 8

Ingredients:

280 g baby spinach leaves
2 tbsp. water
1/4 cup 1% Low-fat cottage cheese
1/4 cup feta cheese, crumbled
2 tbsp. finely grated parmesan cheese
1 egg white
1 tsp. lemon zest
1/4 tsp each, black pepper and kosher salt
1/8 tsp. cayenne pepper
1 tsp. dried oregano

4 sheets frozen phyllo dough, thawed (13x18-inch/13x46-cm)
1 tbsp. olive oil
Cooking spray

Directions:

Heat the Air Fryer to reach 375° Fahrenheit/191° Celsius.
Drain and add the spinach and water to a large pot. Simmer over high heat, stirring often until wilted (5 minutes).
Drain spinach and cool for about 10 minutes. Press firmly using some paper towels to remove as much moisture as possible.
Mix together the spinach, ricotta, feta, Parmesan, egg white, zest, oregano, salt, cayenne, and black pepper in a medium-sized bowl until well combined.
Place a sheet of phyllo on the work surface. Brush lightly with oil making use of a pastry brush. Top with the second sheet of phyllo and brush with oil.
Continue layering to form a stack of four oiled sheets. While working from the longer side, cut the stack of phyllo sheets into eight strips (2 1/4-inch wide). Slice the strips in half, crosswise, to form 16 strips 2 1/4 inches wide.
Pour about a tablespoon of filling onto one short end of each strip. Bend one corner over the filling to create a triangle - keep bending back and forth to the end of the strip, making a triangle-shaped phyllo package.
Lightly coat the fryer basket with cooking spray. Place eight packets seam-side down in the basket. Lightly spray the top. Cook until phyllo is nicely browned (12 min.), flipping packets halfway through the cooking process. Repeat with remaining phyllo packets

Nutrition:

Carbohydrates: 27 g
Fat: 4 g
Protein: 64 g
Calories: 82

103. Vegan-Friendly Kale Chips

Preparation Time: 5 minutes

Cooking Time: 7 minutes

Servings: 2

Ingredients:

1 bunch curly kale
2 tsp. olive oil

1 tbsp. nutritional yeast
1/8 tsp. black pepper
1/4 tsp. sea salt

Directions:

Heat the Air Fryer unit to reach 390°Fahrenheit/199°Celsius.
Thoroughly rinse the kale and pat it dry. Remove the leaves from the stems of the kale and toss them into a mixing container.
Add the olive oil, salt, pepper, and nutritional yeast. Use your hands to massage the toppings into the kale leaves.
Scoop the kale into the basket of the fryer air-fry them until they are crispy (6-7 min.).
Note: If you are using a small Air Fryer, cook the chips in two batches. You don't want to overfill the fryer basket.
Enjoy them piping hot or slightly cooled.
Save any leftover chips in a zip-top bag for up to five days.

Nutrition:

Carbohydrates: 9.1 g
Fat: 5.3 g
Protein: 33.8 g
Calories: 90

104. Light Air-Fried Empanadas

Preparation Time: 10 minutes

Cooking Time: 24 minutes

Servings: 2

Ingredients:

1 tbsp. olive oil
85 g 85/15 lean ground beef
1/4 cup white onion
85 g cremini mushrooms
2 tsp. garlic
6 pitted green olives
1/4 tsp. ground cumin

1/8 tsp. ground cinnamon
1/2 cup tomatoes
8 square gyoza wrappers
1 egg, lightly beaten

Directions:

Heat the Air Fryer unit to reach 400°Fahrenheit/204°Celsius.
Finely chop the onion, mushrooms, olives, and garlic. Also, chop the tomatoes or use canned.
Heat the oil in a skillet using the med-high temperature setting.
Add beef and onion to cook, stirring to crumble until brown (3 min.).
Mix in the mushrooms, occasionally stirring, until the mushrooms start to brown (6 min.).
Toss in the garlic, olives, cumin, and cinnamon cook until mushrooms are very tender and have released most of their liquid (3 min.).
Stir in tomatoes and cook for one minute, stirring intermittently.
Transfer the filling to a holding container and wait for it to cool (5 min.).
Arrange four wrappers on the work surface. Place about 1 1/2 tablespoons of filling in the middle of each wrapper. Brush each of the wrap's edges with egg and fold the wrappers over while pinching its edges to seal.
Repeat the process with the rest of the wrappers and filling.

Place four empanadas in the fryer basket (single-layered), and air-fry at 400°F them until nicely browned (7 min.).

Repeat with the remaining empanadas.

Nutrition:

Carbohydrates: 25 g
Fat: 19 g

Protein: 57 g
Calories: 182

105. Whole-Wheat Air-Fried Pizzas

Preparation Time: 5 minutes

Cooking Time: 4/5 minutes

Servings: 2

2 whole-wheat pita rounds
1 cup baby spinach leaves
1 small plum tomato
1 small garlic clove
1/4 cup pre-shredded part-skim mozzarella cheese
1 tbsp. shaved Parmigiano-Reggiano cheese

Ingredients:

1/4 cup lower-sodium marinara sauce

Directions:

Heat the Air Fryer to 350°Fahrenheit/177°Celsius.
Spread the marinara sauce over one side of each pita bread.
Slice the tomato into eight slices and thinly slice the garlic.
Top each one-off using half of the spinach leaves, tomato slices, garlic, and cheeses.
Place one pita in the fryer basket, and air-fry to 350° F until the cheese is melted and the pita is crispy (4-5 min.).
Repeat with the remaining pita and serve.

Nutrition:

Carbohydrates: 37 g
Fat: 5 g

Protein: 61 g
Calories: 149

106. Zucchini Chips

Preparation Time: 10 minutes

Cooking Time: 12/15 minutes

Servings: 5

Ingredients:

1.5 lb. zucchini
1/2 cup all-purpose flour
1 tsp. Italian seasoning
1/4 cup Parmesan/similar cheese, finely shredded
Black pepper & salt, to taste (very little)
2 eggs
2 cups breadcrumbs
Cooking oil spray, to taste

Directions:

Heat the Air Fryer unit to 400°Fahrenheit/204°Celsius.
Spritz the fryer basket with a tiny bit of cooking oil spray.
Break the eggs and add the flour and breadcrumbs into individual bowls.
Slice the zucchini into chips (1/4-inch thick). Use a mandolin for precise slicing to make the chips close to the same size for even cooking.
Whisk the flour with salt, pepper with a little shredded cheese.
Dip the zucchini pieces in the flour, egg, and lastly, the breadcrumbs before placing them in the fryer basket.
Spray the zucchini chips with cooking oil spray and air-fry for 5 minutes to 400°F.
Open the basket and flip the chips to spritz them with a tiny bit more oil.
Air-fry the zucchini chips until nicely browned (4-7 min.) to serve.

Nutrition: Fat: 4 g Calories: 107 Protein: 69 g Carbohydrates: 31 g

107. Air-Fried Avocado Fries

Preparation Time: 10 minutes

Cooking Time: 7-10 minutes

Servings: 2

Ingredients:

2 tbsp. all-purpose flour
1/8 tsp. salt
1/4 tsp. black pepper
1/2 egg
1/2 tsp. water
1/2 ripe avocado

1/4 cup panko breadcrumbs
Cooking spray

Directions:

Preheat the Air Fryer unit to 400°Fahrenheit/204°Celsius.
Combine flour, pepper, and salt in a small shallow container.
Beat egg and water in a second shallow container. Place panko in a third shallow container.
Cut the avocado in half. Discard the seeds and peel.
Cut the prepared avocado into eight pieces.
Dip one slice of avocado in flour, patting off excess.
Dunk it in the egg and pat out the excess. Finally, press the slice into the panko so both sides are covered.
Place on a platter and replace with the remaining slices.
Generously spray the avocado slices with a cooking oil spray.
Place the slices in the Air Fryer bowl, spray side down. Also, spray the upper side of the avocado slices.
Cook in your pre-heated Air Fryer for 4 minutes to 400°Fahrenheit.
Flip the avocado slices and cook until golden brown (3 minutes).

Nutrition: Protein: 69.3 g Calories: 179 Carbohydrates: 29.8 g Fat: 18 g

108. Chicken Nachos with Pepper

Preparation Time: 10 minutes **Cooking Time:** 7/8 minutes

Servings: 6

Ingredients:

- 1 tbsp bean stew powder
- 1 tsp ground cumin
- 1 tsp salt
- ½ tsp ground dark pepper
- 1 tsp garlic powder
- 1/2 tsp new cleaved cilantro
- 1 pound ground chicken
- 1-pound red chime peppers cut into strips (not spicy)
- 1 ½ cups ground cheddar

Directions:

Preheat your Air Fryer to 400°F.

Combine the flavors in a little bowl.

Add the turkey to an enormous skillet and cook until caramelized. Mix in the zest blend.

Spot the pepper strips in a softly lubed heating container and top with the cooked chicken and cheddar.

Place Air Fryer-safe pan inside and cook for 8 minutes at 400°F or until cheddar has melted and turned brown.

Nutrition:

Calories: 162

Total Fat: 12 g

Total Carbohydrates: 8 g

Protein: 67 g

109. Dark Chocolate and Cranberry Granola Bars

Preparation Time: 10 minutes

Cooking Time: 20 minutes

Servings: 8

Ingredients:

- 1 cup unsweetened shredded coconut
- 1 cup cut almonds
- ½ cup cleaved walnuts
- 1/3 cup dried cranberries
- 1/3 cup unsweetened, dim chocolate chips
- ½ cup hemp seeds
- ½ tsp salt
- ½ cup margarine
- 2 tsp keto maple syrup
- ½ cup powdered erythritol
- ½ tsp vanilla

Directions:

Preheat your Air Fryer to 300°F and line the Air Fryer plate with cooking paper.

Add the coconut, nuts, and hemp seeds to a food processor and pulse until very much blended and brittle.

Spot the blend in an enormous bowl alongside the cranberries, dull chocolate chips, and salt.

In a little pot, dissolve the margarine and maple syrup over low warmth.

Rush in the erythritol and mix until softened. Increase the heat and add the vanilla concentrate.

Pour the margarine blend over the nut blend and mix rapidly to cover uniformly.

Pour the blend onto the readied sheet plate and press down so the blend is leveled and even. Attempt to reduce it however much as could reasonably be expected so the bars hold together well.

Place the dish in the Air Fryer and bake for 20 minutes to 300°F. The edges should turn marginally brown.

Cool the bars totally and afterward cut and serve!

Nutrition:

Calories: 149

Total Fat: 12 g

Total Carbohydrates: 6 g

Protein: 63 g

110. Bacon Muffin Bites

Preparation Time: 20 minutes

Cooking Time: 25 minutes

Servings: 24 little biscuits

Ingredients:

2 cups almond flour
1 cup coconut flour
2 tsp preparing powder
1 cup destroyed cheddar
½ cup margarine
1/4 cup cleaved parsley
1/2 cup cooked, chopped bacon
Salt, to taste (very little)
6 tbsp liquefied spread
1/4 cup minced garlic
1/2 cup acrid cream
4 eggs

Directions:

Preheat your Air Fryer to 325°F and shower little biscuit tin or individual small-scale biscuit cups with cooking spray.

In a pan, over medium-high heat, cook the bacon, 5 to 7 minutes, flipping too evenly crisp. Dry out on paper towels, crumble, and set aside.

Spot the harsh cream, 1 tbsp garlic, eggs, and salt in a food processor, and puree until smooth.

Add the flours, cheddar, and parsley to the food processor and puree until a smooth mixture structure.

Overlap in the bacon chopped.

Melt the margarine

Distribute the mixture into the cookie cups.

Join the liquefied margarine and the leftover garlic and afterward brush the highest points of every biscuit with the spread blend.

Place the cookies in the deep fryer and bake for 18 minutes at 325°F or until the tops are bright earthy colored.

Cool before serving and appreciate!

Nutrition:

Calories: 128
Total Fat: 1 g
Total Carbohydrates: 5 g
Protein: 42 g

111. Brussels Sprout Chips

Preparation Time: 10 minutes

Cooking Time: 15 minutes

Servings: 4

Ingredients:

1 pound Brussels sprouts, closes eliminated

2 tbsp. olive oil
1 tsp ocean salt

Directions:

Preheat your Air Fryer to 240°F and line the Air Fryer plate with cooking paper.

Strip the Brussels sprouts each leaf in turn, setting the leaves in a huge bowl as you strip them.

Throw the leaves with olive oil and salt and afterward spread on the readied plate.

Place in the Air Fryer and cook for 15 minutes at 240°F, putting a little at a time to cook evenly.

Nutrition:

Calories: 104
Total Fat: 7 g
Total Carbohydrates: 9 g
Protein: 33 g

112. Herbed Parmesan Crackers

Preparation Time: 25 minutes

Cooking Time: 45 minutes

Servings: 10

Ingredients:

1 ½ cups sunflower seeds
3/4 cup parmesan cheddar, ground
2 tbsp Italian flavoring
1/2 cup chia seeds
1/2 tsp garlic powder
1/2 tsp heating powder

1 egg
2 tbsp. margarine, liquefied
Salt, to taste (very little)

Directions:

Preheat your Air Fryer to 300°F.
Spot the sunflower seeds and chia seeds in a food processor until finely mixed into a powder. Spot in a huge bowl.
Add the cheddar, Italian flavoring, garlic powder, and preparing powder to the bowl and blend well.
Include the liquefied margarine and egg and mix until a pleasant mixture structure.
Spot the batter on a piece of cooking paper and afterward place another piece of cooking paper on top.
Fold the batter into a meager sheet around 1/8 inches thick.
Discard the top piece of paper towel and lift the batter using the base paper towel and place it on a plate that fits in the fryer.
Using the mixture, create the shape of crackers you want and place them in the Air Fryer to cook for 40-45 minutes at 300°F.
Split the saltines up and appreciate!

Nutrition:

Calories: 173
Total Fat: 18 g
Total Carbohydrates: 9 g
Protein: 39 g

113. Cauliflower Crunch

Preparation Time: 5 minutes

Cooking Time: 20/30 minutes

Ingredients:

4 cups cauliflower florets, chopped into scaled-down pieces

Servings: 4

1 tbsp olive oil
1 tsp ocean salt

Directions:

Preheat your Air Fryer to 135°F.
Wash and channel the cauliflower florets.

Spot the cauliflower in a big bowl and throw with the olive oil and ocean salt.

Add the cauliflower to the bushel of your Air Fryer or spread them in a level layer on the plate of your Air Fryer (either alternative will work!).

Cook in the Air Fryer for around 20/30 minutes to 135°F, turning the cauliflower consistently to cook uniformly. Basically, you will dry out the cauliflower.

When the cauliflower is completely dried, eliminate it from the Air Fryer and afterward let cool. It will stay fresh as it cools.

Appreciate fresh or store in an impenetrable compartment for as long as a month.

Nutrition:

Calories: 55
Total Fat: 3 g
Total Carbohydrates: 4 g
Protein: 31 g

114. Lemon Pepper Broccoli Crunch

Preparation Time: 5 minutes

Cooking Time: 15/20 minutes

Servings: 4

Ingredients:

- 4 cups broccoli florets, slashed into reduced down pieces
- 1 tbsp olive oil
- 1 tsp ocean salt
- 1 tsp lemon pepper preparing

Directions:

Preheat your Air Fryer to 135°F.

Wash and channel the broccoli florets.

Spot the broccoli in an enormous bowl and throw it with the olive oil and ocean salt.

Add the broccoli to the container of your Air Fryer or spread them in a level layer on the plate of your Air Fryer (either choice will work!).

Cook in the Air Fryer for around 15/20 minutes to 135°F, turning the broccoli consistently to cook equitably. Basically, you will get dried out the broccoli.

When the broccoli is completely dried, take it out from the Air Fryer, throw with the lemon pepper preparing, and afterward let cool. It will stay fresh as it cools.

Appreciate fresh or store in a hermetically sealed compartment for as long as a month.

Nutrition:

Calories: 53
Total Fat: 3 g
Net Carbohydrates: 1 g
Protein: 52 g

115. Delicate Garlic Parmesan Pretzels

Preparation Time: 15 minutes

Cooking Time: 12/14 minutes

Servings: 6

Ingredients:

- 2 cups almond flour
- 1 tbsp preparing powder
- 1 tsp garlic powder
- 1 tsp onion powder
- 3 eggs
- 5 tbsp mollified cream cheddar
- 3 cups mozzarella cheddar, ground
- 1 tsp ocean salt
- ½ tsp garlic powder
- ¼ cup parmesan cheddar

Directions:

Preheat your Air Fryer to 400°F and set up the Air Fryer plate with cooking paper.

Spot the almond flour, onion powder, preparing powder, and 1 tsp garlic powder in a big bowl and mix well.

Join the cream cheddar and mozzarella in a different bowl and dissolve in the microwave, warming gradually and mixing a few times to guarantee the cheddar liquefies and doesn't consume.

Add two eggs to the almond flour blend alongside the dissolved cheddar. Mix well until a mixture forms.

Separate the batter into six equivalent pieces and fold into your ideal pretzel shape.

Spot the pretzels on the readied sheet plate.

Whisk the excess eggs and brush over the pretzels, at that point sprinkle them all with the ocean salt, parmesan, and 1/2 tsp garlic powder.

Cook in the Air Fryer for 12 minutes to 400°F or until the pretzels are brilliant earthy colored.

Remove from Air Fryer and appreciate it.

Nutrition:

Calories: 193
Total Fat: 39 g
Total Carbohydrates: 10 g
Protein: 48 g

116. Cucumber Chips

Preparation Time: 15 minutes

Cooking Time: 15 minutes

Servings: 4

Ingredients:

4 cups dainty cucumber cuts
2 tbsp apple juice vinegar
2 tsp ocean salt

Directions:

Preheat your Air Fryer to 200°F.

Spot the cucumber cuts on a paper towel and layer another paper towel on top to ingest the dampness in the cucumbers.

Spot the dried cuts in a huge bowl and throw with the vinegar and salt.

Place the cucumber cuts on a plate secured with paper towels and then cook in the fryer for 15 minutes to 200°F. The cucumbers will begin to twist and brown a bit.

Turn off the Air Fryer and let the cucumber cuts cool inside the fryer (this will help them dry somewhat more).

Appreciate immediately or store in an impermeable holder.

Nutrition:

Calories: 15
Total Fat: 0 g
Total Carbohydrates: 4 g
Protein: 31 g

Chapter 8. Dessert Recipes

117. Chocolate Mug Cake

Preparation Time: 7 minutes

Cooking Time: 13 minutes

Servings: 3

Ingredients:

½ cup of cocoa powder
½ cup stevia powder
1 cup coconut cream
1 package cream cheese, room temperature
1 tbsp. vanilla extract
1 tbsp. butter

Directions:

Smart Air Fryer Oven is prepared at 350°F for a further 5 minutes.
Using a hand mixer, blend all the mentioned ingredients until frothy.
Put them into fatty cups.
In the fryer basket, place the cups and bake at 350°F for 13 minutes.
Serve as cold as possible.

Nutrition:

Calories: 100
Fat: 0 g
Carbohydrates: 21 g
Sugar 6 g
Protein: 3 g

118. Chocolate Soufflé

Preparation Time: 7 minutes

Cooking Time: 12 minutes

Servings: 2

Ingredients:

1 tbsp. Almond flour
½ tsp. vanilla
1 tbsp. sweetener
2 separated eggs
¼ cups melted coconut oil
4 oz. of semi-sweet chocolate, chopped

Directions:

Preheat the Smart Air Fryer Oven to 330°F.
Brush coconut oil and sweetener onto ramekins.
Melt coconut oil and chocolate together.
Beat egg yolks well, adding vanilla and sweetener.
Stir in flour and ensure there are no lumps.
Whisk egg whites till they reach peak state and fold them into chocolate mixture.
Pour batter into ramekins and place into the Smart Air Fryer Oven, then cook for 12 minutes.
Serve with powdered sugar dusted on top.

Nutrition:

Calories: 612
Fat: 43g
Carbohydrates: 46g
Protein: 9g

119. Chocolate Cake

Preparation Time: 6 minutes

Cooking Time: 35 minutes

Servings: 9

Ingredients:

½ cups hot water
1 tsp. vanilla
¼ cups olive oil
½ cups almond milk
1 egg
½ tsp. Salt
¾ tsp. baking soda
¾ tsp. baking powder
½ cups unsweetened cocoa powder
2 cups almond flour
1 cup brown sugar

Directions:

Turn the Smart Air Fryer Oven to 356°F.
Mix the dry ingredients and then stir in the wet.
Add hot water last.
The thin batter is better.
Bake a cake batter-sized pan in the fryer.
Bake for 35 minutes.

Nutrition:

214 calories
Protein: 3.2g
Carbohydrates: 25.5g
Fat: 11.7g
Cholesterol: 73.2mg
Sodium: 130.3mg

120. Choc Chip Air Fryer Cookies

Preparation Time: 10 minutes

Cooking Time: 16 minutes

Servings: 3

Ingredients:

75 g brown sugar
75 g milk chocolate
30 milliliters honey
30 milliliters whole milk
75 g self raising flour
100 g butter

Directions:

Beat the butter until smooth and fluffy.
Add the butter to the sugar and beat together in a smooth mixture.
Now add and mix in the milk, sugar, chocolate (broken into small chunks/chips), and flour.
Preheat your Air Fryer to 360F.
Form the mixture into cookie shapes and place on a baking sheet that will rest in the Air Fryer for 16 minutes. Use (heat) the oven.

Nutrition:

Calories: 179
Fat: 9g
Carbohydrates: 22g
Protein: 2g
Cholesterol: 23 mg

Conclusion

Diabetes is a serious condition caused by a deficiency of insulin. Insulin is a hormone that is necessary for the proper functioning of the body. When a person develops diabetes, the cells in the body do not respond to insulin properly. The result is that the cells do not get the energy and nutrients they need, and then they start to die.

Being diagnosed with diabetes will bring some major changes in your lifestyle. From the time you are diagnosed with it, it would always be a constant battle with the food. You need to become a lot more careful with your food choices and the quantity that you ate. Every meal will feel like a major effort. You will be planning every day for the whole week, well in advance. Depending upon the type of food you ate, you have to keep checking your blood sugar levels. You may get used to taking long breaks between meals and staying away from snacks between dinner and breakfast.

Food would be treated as a bomb like it can go off at any time. According to an old saying, "When the body gets too hot, then your body heads straight to the kitchen."

Managing diabetes can be a very, very stressful ordeal. There will be many times that you will mark your glucose levels down on a piece of paper like you are plotting graph lines or something. You will mix your insulin shots up and then stress about whether or not you are giving yourself the right dosage. You will always be over-cautious because it involves a lot of math and a really fine margin of error. But now, those days are gone!

With the help of technology and books, you can stock your kitchen with the right foods, like meal plans, diabetic friendly dishes, etc. You can also get an app that will even do the work for you. You can also people-watch on the internet and find the know-how to cook and eat right; you will always be a few meals away from certain disasters, like a plummeting blood sugar level. Always carry some sugar in your pocket. You won't have to experience the pangs of hunger but if you are unlucky, you will have to ration your food and bring along some simple low-calorie snacks with you.

This is the future of diabetes.

As you've reached the end of this book, you have gained complete control of your diabetes and this is just the beginning of your journey towards a better, healthier life. I hope I was able to inculcate some knowledge into you and make this adventure a little bit less of a struggle.

I would like to remind you that you're not alone in having to manage this disease and that nearly 85 % of the new cases are 20 years old or younger.

Regardless of the length or seriousness of your diabetes, it can be managed! Take the information presented here and start with it!

Preparation is key to having a healthier and happier life.

It's helpful to remember that every tool at your disposal can help in some way.

Index

A

Air Fryer Brussels Sprouts; 80
Air-Fried Avocado Fries; 122
Almond Crust Chicken; 25
Apple Chips With Cinnamon and Yogurt Sauce; 115
Asparagus; 90
Asparagus & Parmesan; 84
Asparagus Salad; 30

B

Bacon Muffin Bites; 125
Bacon-Wrapped Filet Mignon; 32; 41
BBQ Pork Chops; 44
BBQ Pork Ribs; 48
Beef Burgers; 53
Breaded Coconut Shrimp; 100
Breaded Cod; 73
Brine-Soaked Turkey; 56
Brussels Sprout Chips; 126
Buttered Salmon; 63
Buttery Cod; 99

C

Cauliflower Crunch; 128
Cauliflower Steak; 92
Chard with Cheddar; 86
Chicken & Zucchini Omelet; 19
Chicken Drumsticks; 59
Chicken Nachos with Pepper; 123
Chicken Omelet; 23

Choc Chip Air Fryer Cookies; 135
Chocolate Cake; 134
Chocolate Mug Cake; 132
Chocolate Soufflé; 133
Classic Beef Jerky; 42
Cod and Chicken Broth; 111
Codfish Nuggets; 101
Creamy Cabbage; 83
Creamy Potatoes; 82
Crispy Haddock; 64
Crispy Meatballs; 45
Crispy Tilapia; 68
Crunchy Air Fryer Fish; 97
Crusted Chicken Drumsticks; 70
Cucumber Chips; 131

D

Dark Chocolate and Cranberry Granola Bars; 124
Deep-Fried Prawns; 105
Delicate Garlic Parmesan Pretzels; 130
Delicious Air Fryer Cauliflower; 76

E

Easy Beef Roast; 38
Easy Crab Sticks; 102
Easy Italian Meatballs; 62
Easy Prawn Salad; 108
Easy Rosemary Lamb Chops; 36
Eggplant Parmigiana; 79
Endives with Bacon Mix; 81

F

Flavorful Steak; 43

Fried Catfish; 103

Fried Fish Fingers; 109

G

Garlic Potatoes with Bacon; 18

Greek Lamb Chops; 37

Green Beans and Cherry Tomatoes; 94

Grilled Sardines; 96

Ground Chicken Meatballs; 66

H

Herb Butter Rib-Eye Steak; 49

Herbed Parmesan Crackers; 127

Herbed Tomatoes; 87

Honey Mustard Pork Tenderloin; 50

J

Juicy Pork Chops; 39

Juicy Steak Bites; 46

L

Leeks; 89

Lemon Chicken Breasts; 60

Lemon Garlic Lamb Chops; 47

Lemon Pepper Broccoli Crunch; 129

Lemony Lentils with "Fried" Onions; 91

Lemony Raspberries Bowls; 29

Lemony Salmon; 67

Light Air-Fried Empanadas; 119

M

Miso Glazed Salmon; 65

Monkfish with Olives and Capers; 106

Mozzarella Cheese Bites with Marinara Sauce; 116

Mushroom Cheese Salad; 26

Mushrooms and Cheese Spread; 28

O

Onion Green Beans; 93

Onion Omelet; 34

Onion Soup; 95

Oregano Chicken Breast; 57

P

Parmesan Chicken Meatballs; 61

Pumpkin Pancakes; 33

S

Salmon with Mushrooms and Bell Pepper; 110

Salmon with Pistachio Bark; 107

Scrambled Eggs; 24

Season and Salt-Cured Beef; 54

Seasoned Beef Roast; 52

Shrimp Frittata; 21

Shrimp Sandwiches; 27

Simple Beef Patties; 55

Simple Beef Sirloin Roast; 51

Simple Haddock; 72

Spanakopita Bites; 117

Spiced Almonds; 88

Spiced Tilapia; 71

Spicy Catfish; 74

Spinach Quiche; 77

Spinach with Tuna Fish; 112

Strawberries Oatmeal; 16

Sweet Potato with Tilapia; 113

Sweetened Breakfast Oats; 35

T

Tacos Crispy Avocado; 114

Thyme Turkey Breast; 58

Tomatoes and Swiss Chard Bake; 20

Tuna and Spring Onions Salad; 40

Tuna Burgers; 75

Tuna Sandwiches; 17

Tuna Zucchini Melts; 98

V

Vegan-Friendly Kale Chips; 118

Vinegar Halibut; 69

W

Walnut & Cheese Filled Mushrooms; 85

Whole-Wheat Air-Fried Pizzas; 120

Y

Yellow Squash Fritters; 78

Z

Zucchini Chips; 121

Zucchini Fritters; 22

Zucchini Squash Mix; 31

Zucchini with Tuna; 104

Made in the USA
Columbia, SC
03 April 2023